"Nick Wagner has once again written a practical and insightful book for those directing or supporting the RCIA in a parish. This book provides RCIA teams and directors with a place to start, where to go, and a good idea of what seekers need. Nick is a great storyteller and this book is rich with stories that enlighten and inform us. In particular, the parallel he draws between the demise of the steel industry and what we do in RCIA is thought provoking and accurate. The importance of the Kerygma is central to this book as Nick leads the reader through an uncomplicated core content focused on Jesus and aimed at making not just Catholics but 'Catholic Disciples.'"

> — Cathy Marbury
> Associate Director of Religious Education
> Archdiocese of Atlanta

"Starting from the ground up is just what Nick Wagner does in his newest book. Our RCIA processes have become encumbered by false understandings that the 'program' needs to be a graduate course in theology, and not about a time of catechesis on changing hearts for living the life of a disciple of Christ: a process. So often our contemporary Church is lured away from the wisdom of lived experience by the newest and shiniest 'program' on how to enliven our parishes. Nick starts with what the Church teaches, and he stays the course regarding his solid experience on presenting the richness of the RCIA process for changing hearts. Nick lays out the fact that the RCIA process is not about knowledge only, but about discipleship."

> — Dean Daniels
> Office for Worship
> Archdiocese of Milwaukee

Field Hospital Catechesis

The Core Content for RCIA Formation

Nick Wagner

LITURGICAL PRESS

Collegeville, Minnesota

www.litpress.org

1   2   3   4   5   6   7   8   9

Library of Congress Control Number: 2017957154

ISBN 978-0-8146-4466-9   ISBN 978-0-8146-4489-8 (e-book)

Contents

Chapter 1

Disrupting the Church

Clayton Christensen, author of *The Innovator's Dilemma*, likes to tell business leaders the story of the transformation of the steel industry:

> Most of the world's steel has been made by massive integrated steel companies. The other way to do it is to build a mini mill. In a mini mill, you melt scrap in electric furnaces, and you could easily fit four of them in this room. The most important thing about a mini mill is that you can make steel for twenty per cent lower cost than you can make it in an integrated mill. Now, imagine you're the C.E.O. of a steel company somewhere. In a really good year, your net profit will be two to four per cent. (quoted in Larissa MacFarquhar, "When Giants Fail," *The New Yorker*)

So if you were that CEO, wouldn't you immediately switch your business to a mini mill model? No, you would not. According to Christensen, not a single integrated steel company, anywhere in the world, has built a mini mill. "Today, all but one of the integrated mills have gone bankrupt," said Christensen.

1

On first hearing this story, you might think the managers are stupid. Or overly cautious. Or just resistant to change. But think about that for a minute. These are the leaders of what had been some of the most powerful, most profitable companies in the history of the world. You don't get to a level like that by accident.

Christensen's analysis of the situation is that the leaders of the big steel companies did exactly the right thing—according to their worldview. The problem is they had a faulty worldview. Actually, it was more than a worldview. Christensen called it a "near-religion," the "Church of New Finance."

What Does the Steel Industry Have to Do with Faith Formation?

About now, you may be wondering what this has to do with RCIA ministry. Or maybe you've guessed already. Many of us have a worldview—even a "near-religion"—about how RCIA is supposed to work. And, like the big integrated steel mills, many of our RCIA processes are in trouble. So stick with me a minute as we look more closely at what happened to big steel and the lesson we can learn for our formation processes.

Christensen discovered that every business sector has a "near-religion" worldview that blinds it to new ways of doing things. Everywhere we turn, new technologies arise that disrupt big, established companies. And here's the weird part. These new technologies are often discovered or developed by the big companies themselves. But they are deemed too inferior in quality or profit potential to be worth the time to invest in. So a smaller upstart company takes over the "low" end of the market, eventually growing big enough to disrupt its larger competitors. Here's how it worked in the steel industry.

The first builders of mini mills would make steel by melting down scrap metal. The only thing their product was good for was making the steel rods that reinforced concrete: rebar. Rebar is the lowest tier of the steel market, and the profit margin is very low. The big steel companies were happy to have someone else make rebar. They could then drop their lowest tier offering and focus on higher quality, higher profit-making products, like the sheet metal used in car manufacturing.

However, as the mini mills got better at what they did, they set their sights on the next lowest level of big steel's market and started producing that at rates the big companies couldn't match. And the trend continued, bit by bit, with the mini mills climbing up from the bottom and the big companies moving higher and higher upmarket. The trend continued until the mini mills had almost the total market and most of the bigger companies declared bankruptcy.

The "Nones" Are Disrupting Christianity

As church leaders, we can learn a lesson from the story of the steel mills. Our sector—Christianity—is being disrupted. The number of people in the United States who claim to be religiously unaffiliated—the "nones"—is larger than either the number of Catholics or the number of mainline Protestants. And yet, the nones report having a deep feeling of "spirituality." Someone is making spiritual rebar and offering more attractive options than our big, integrated religious institutions can.

The bishops of the Catholic Church are not oblivious to this trend. Like the CEOs of big steel, you don't get to be a bishop by being out of touch. In 2012, the bishops of the world met as a synod to advise Pope Benedict XVI about the needs of the church. Pope Benedict stepped down before the propositions of the synod could be acted upon, and it was left to Pope Francis to carry them out.

Proposition 7 proposed that "the Church proclaim the permanent world-wide missionary dimension of her mission in order to encourage all the particular Churches to evangelize." This is akin to the leaders of big steel saying we have to make more steel. Proposition 8 recognized the influence of secular culture. The bishops said, "As Christians we cannot remain indifferent to the process of secularization. We are in fact in a situation similar to that of the first Christians and as such we should see this both as a challenge and a possibility." This is similar to the steel CEOs recognizing the threat of the mini mills and resolving to address it.

Proposition 9 says, "The 'first proclamation' is where the kerygma, the message of salvation of the paschal mystery of Jesus Christ, is proclaimed with great spiritual power." And closely linked is Proposition 10, which says, "It is an inalienable right for each person, whatever one's religion or lack of religion, to be able to know Jesus Christ and the Gospel. This proclamation, given with integrity, must be offered with a total respect for each person, without any form of proselytizing."

How to Not Get Disrupted

To me, these last two propositions are the key to solving our disruption problem. If we can recognize the challenge and possibility of increased secularization (proposition 8) and become truly missionary (proposition 7), we will become a dynamic church instead of a disrupted church. We have to proclaim the spiritually powerful message that Jesus offers salvation to everyone, and we have to do it with total respect for each person, without proselytizing.

But there is a big hurdle, much like the hurdle faced by the big, integrated steel companies. While the big companies were capable of turning out rebar, their focus and passion was upmarket—producing high-quality sheet metal. In a similar way, our big, integrated church is capable of announcing the simple "first proclamation" that Jesus offers salvation to all. And yet, much of our institutional effort is still focused "upmarket," offering sophisticated theological teachings and religious practices designed to meet the needs of the most active members of our parishes.

Just as the big steel CEOs had a worldview, a "near-religion," that kept them focused on the high-profit products, most parish leaders today have an actual religion that is focused on the already-religious. It is almost impossible to imagine disrupting the current situation to build "mini mills" in the middle of our parishes.

And yet, almost as soon as he was elected and every day since, that is exactly what Pope Francis has been exhorting us to do.

Chapter 2

Why the Teaching of the Church Is at Risk

Pope Francis is trying to get the church to focus on building "spiritual mini mills" before we get disrupted. We cannot continue with a "business as usual" attitude. Francis said, "There's a phrase that should never be used: 'It's always been done that way.' That phrase, let me tell you, is bad. We must always be changing because time changes" (Rome Reports).

In response to the 2012 bishops' synod, Pope Francis set out a plan for change. In Joy of the Gospel, he said that our primary job is to evangelize. Now, all the popes since Pope Paul VI in the 1970s have been saying this. But so far, our focus has remained "upmarket," ministering to those of us who have already been evangelized.

Pope Francis insists that we focus on evangelization not just because that teaching is in line with a long tradition of the church, dating back to Jesus's last words to his disciples (see Matt 28:18-20). The pope sees a real danger in the world:

> The great danger in today's world, pervaded as it is by consumerism, is the desolation and anguish born of a complacent yet

covetous heart, the feverish pursuit of frivolous pleasures, and a blunted conscience. (Joy of the Gospel, 2)

To evangelize is to literally announce good news. Sometimes, however, we can get so caught up in all the details of the Good News that we turn it into boring news. Or even worse, we turn it into daunting news, a list of doctrines and precepts that must be assented to before one can be saved. Pope Francis is telling us we have to focus on the essentials of the faith.

The Essential Truths

All of church teaching flows from the same source—the God of truth. But some truths are more important than others in the work of evangelization. When we are reaching out to those who have deep wounds, whose lives are in darkness, who truly have no hope, we have to focus on the most essential truths, the heart of the Gospel. Pope Francis said,

> The thing the church needs most today is the ability to heal wounds and to warm the hearts of the faithful; it needs nearness, proximity. I see the church as a field hospital after battle. It is useless to ask a seriously injured person if he has high cholesterol and about the level of his blood sugars! You have to heal his wounds. Then we can talk about everything else. Heal the wounds, heal the wounds. (Spadaro, "A Big Heart Open to God," *America*)

In Joy of the Gospel, Pope Francis says that what counts above all else is "faith working through love" (Gal 5:6). In other words, we have to learn to evangelize by doing works of love. And of all the ways we can express love for our neighbor, Francis says that mercy is the greatest way in which we can manifest God's love to others.

In *The Name of God Is Mercy*, Pope Francis tells the story he read in a novel of a World War II German soldier sentenced to death. The protagonist of the novel, young Father Gaston, needs to hear the confession of the soldier. In addition to his other crimes, the soldier is guilty of "numerous amorous adventures." He is sorry for the crimes that led to his death sentence, but of his love of women, the soldier says to his confessor, "How can I repent? It was something that I enjoyed, and if I had the chance I would do it again, even now. How can I repent?" The priest is desperate to absolve the condemned prisoner and, in a burst of inspiration, asks the soldier, "But are you sorry that you are not sorry?" The soldier replies immediately, "Yes, I am sorry that I am not sorry" (xix–xx).

That crack in the door, being sorry for not being sorry, is all the Spirit needs to flood us with grace and mercy. It is the deluge of God's mercy that heals the wounds of the world.

For most of us, the seekers we encounter will not be condemned prisoners. Their "condemnation" will be more hidden and subtle. It may even be self-imposed. Our challenge is to be open to every encounter with a seeker and see those encounters as opportunities to offer God's mercy and healing.

Super Healer

In 2009, Jan DeBlieu's sixteen-year-old son was killed in a car accident. It is impossible to imagine the agonizing pain, the bleakness of days that followed, the emptiness of life after that. A loss like that would leave most of us devastated and incapacitated.

And that was true for DeBlieu as well. But, as time moved relentlessly forward, the horror of her tragedy gradually faded, the rawness of her emotions dulled into the background. And now she has what she calls a superpower. Whenever she sees someone else in pain, her pain comes flooding right back, full force:

The question then becomes how I respond. Do I allow these
feelings to overwhelm me, and retreat into the dark sorrow
I know so well? Sometimes, yes, I do. But more often—I've
been working hard on this—I try to stand silently for a moment, letting myself feel the other person's pain. I ask myself
if there's something I can do to help.

She says the best thing she can do for a person in pain is to
listen, to stay with that person until her heart tells her it is okay
to leave. "All this can be a powerful balm for someone who's
having a terrible moment, or a terrible day," she says. "I know
from experience."

But having a superpower is not the same as being super-
human. She has busy days and times when she's distracted.
"Often I'll see a person in need and speed right by," she says.
"The world is full of pain. I can't take it all on."

DeBlieu doesn't go out looking for people in pain. She
spends her days pretty much the same way everyone does.
But she does make an effort to be aware of her surroundings
and keep an openness about herself, being willing to engage
others she encounters during the day:

> Grief has taught me that I can reach out, if only I dare. This is
> the source of my "superpower": The willingness to look at
> suffering full on, without flinching. We'd rather not be con-
> fronted by deep pain in this culture. We'd rather keep it hid-
> den, and hide it within ourselves. But by hiding it, we imprison
> ourselves in the loneliest kind of solitary confinement.

She says reaching out, being open to others, makes her feel
liberated. She now wields her immensely healing "superpower"
by saying three simple words: "Can I help?" ("Using Your Grief
to Help Others—and Heal Yourself," *The Huffington Post*).

Getting the Proportions Right

If we believe what the pope is telling us about the necessity of healing wounds and offering God's mercy, then the content of our evangelization becomes very important. We have to have a sense of proportion. We have to give more emphasis to what Jesus had to say about mercy, love, and justice. We would not spend the bulk of our time talking about sin and judgment. We would spend a lot of time talking about grace and less time talking about the law. We would focus more on the person of Jesus Christ than on the institution of the church. Pope Francis says,

> If this invitation [to life in Jesus Christ] does not radiate forcefully and attractively, the edifice of the Church's moral teaching risks becoming a house of cards, and this is our greatest risk.
>
> It would mean that it is not the Gospel which is being preached, but certain doctrinal or moral points based on specific ideological options. The message will run the risk of losing its freshness and will cease to have "the fragrance of the Gospel." (Joy of the Gospel, 39)

We cannot miss the opportunity to speak to those who are truly wounded. All of the teaching of the church is true, and all of it is important. But the deeper and more nuanced teachings of the church are all at the service of the core teaching. The bulk of what we find in the *Catechism of the Catholic Church* is meant to shine the spotlight on the central message of the Gospel—which could easily fit on one page of the Catechism.

Theologians call this core teaching the kerygma. Kerygma comes from a Greek word that means proclamation. In the sense it is used in Scripture, kerygma means the proclamation of an event. And for Christians, the event we proclaim is Jesus Christ. Pope Francis describes the character of this proclamation in Joy of the Gospel:

> On the lips of the catechist the first proclamation must ring out over and over: "Jesus Christ loves you; he gave his life to save you; and now he is living at your side every day to enlighten, strengthen and free you." (164)

If you are on an RCIA team, or if you are involved in any kind of faith formation, or even if you are only a baptized Christian who takes faith seriously, I would challenge you to pray over that sentence. Why do you think the pope wrote about the kerygma in that way? What does it mean to you, personally? How would you actually implement the pope's directive? What would happen if you did?

When seekers approach us asking what they have to do to become Catholic, most RCIA teams respond by enrolling them in school. We have a syllabus and lesson plans that are either drawn directly from the *Catechism of the Catholic Church* or from resources based on the Catechism.

In *Becoming Catholic*, sociologist David Yamane tells the story of Deacon Zeke, the coordinator of adult religious education for a parish in the Midwest. Professor Yamane sat in on several of Deacon Zeke's classes for people participating in the *Rite of Christian Initiation of Adults* and noted that for 90 percent of the time, Zeke lectured from a diocesan approved "comprehensive catechesis for the RCIA." When he did ask an occasional question, Zeke did not seem to expect a response from the participants. "He fills in the dead spaces himself with more lecturing," said Yamane. The participants, as one might expect, "are not visibly responsive: no acknowledgement of what he is saying with facial expressions, nods of the head, or audible confirmations" (104).

The motivation behind this method is good—we want seekers to deeply and completely understand what it means to be Catholic.

The result, however, is often not so good. Very often, seekers are looking for love or salvation or enlightenment or strength or liberation—all of which they will find in the person of Jesus Christ. And very often, we skip right over that core message so that we can get to the "meat" of church teaching. Like big steel, we turn "upmarket" and forgo focusing on the basics of the faith. As a result, seekers often are never really introduced to Jesus and do not develop a relationship with the risen Christ. They may end up knowing a lot about Catholicism, but they never end up really knowing Jesus.

What Will Happen If We Do This

If, as catechists and ministers of formation, we can keep ourselves focused on the core message, two things will happen.

First, we will experience a deep renewal in our own faith. The core message of our faith is that Jesus loves us. How can we ever tire of hearing that? How much would our own love of Christ grow if we focused on that message every day? How much stronger would we be if, in response to every blessing and every challenge, we knew we were never alone? And then, how much more confident and effective would we be as mentors for others who are just beginning to hear the message that Jesus loves them?

Second, we will witness deep and powerful conversion in our seekers. Most of the time, seekers are not actually asking to be Catholic or to be baptized or to celebrate confirmation or the Eucharist. They are longing for something deep and meaningful. Sometimes they need to be healed of something. Because they don't yet have a strong relationship with Jesus, they don't really know what to ask for. So they tend to ask for things they think will meet their deep need. Maybe if I become Catholic, they think, my life will be better.

That's true! But only if they first hear and understand that initial proclamation—the event of Jesus loving them. Pope Francis says,

> The centrality of the kerygma calls for stressing those elements which are most needed today: it has to express God's saving love which precedes any moral and religious obligation on our part; it should not impose the truth but appeal to freedom; it should be marked by joy, encouragement, liveliness and a harmonious balance which will not reduce preaching to a few doctrines which are at times more philosophical than evangelical. (Joy of the Gospel, 165)

The centrality of the kerygma, what Pope Francis calls the "first proclamation," is what we explore in this book. Before we begin, however, I would ask you to take up the challenge I offered earlier.

Spend some time in prayer over Francis's description of the first proclamation:

> Jesus Christ loves you; he gave his life to save you; and now he is living at your side every day to enlighten, strengthen and free you.

Chapter 3

Where Do We Learn the Core Message?

If Jesus is the core message we must teach, the core story we must tell, where and how do we learn about Jesus?

We might be tempted to say that we turn first to the Scriptures, specifically the gospels, to learn the story of Jesus. Some might even say the *Catechism of the Catholic Church* or other church documents. As important as these sources are, however, they are not the primary ways in which we encounter the risen Christ.

Knowing Scripture is Not Enough

If you recall the story of the disciples on the road to Emmaus, they knew the Scriptures by heart. They knew what the rabbis had written and taught about the Messiah. And yet, it was only an encounter with the risen Christ in the breaking of the bread where they discovered Jesus. They understood only when Jesus revealed himself in the Eucharist.

Neither the Scriptures nor the teaching of the church, by themselves, are sufficient to reveal the fullness of Christ to seekers. Liturgical scholar Goffredo Boselli wrote in *The Spiritual Meaning of the Liturgy*,

> According to the Easter stories of the evangelist Luke, the texts of Scripture are not enough to arouse the disciples' faith in Jesus'

resurrection; it is, rather, the Risen One who, manifesting himself to the eleven, "opened their minds to understand the scriptures" (Luke 24:45). (9)

That is because the risen Christ is mystery. Christ is not mystery in the sense of a difficult puzzle. Christ is mystery like the mystery of love. Boselli describes the Christian understanding of mystery:

> But in the third and fourth centuries, in places rich in Greek culture . . . [t]he fathers did not assume the Greek concept of mystery, since for the Greeks mystery was a reality that had to remain hidden and of which one could not speak. The Greek understanding of mystery, then, is exactly the opposite of the Judeo-Christian one, for which the mystery is the revelation of the secret of God and God's will. (7)

In our own faith experience, just as in the Emmaus story, Christ is the one who opens our hearts and minds to know him. Jesus's entire mission was to reveal the mystery, the secret of God's will. Jesus is a mystagogue. He is a mystagogue for the first disciples who, in turn, become mystagogues for those they initiate into the mystery (see Boselli, 8). And following in their tradition, we are mystagogues for those we initiate into the mystery of Christ.

In the Emmaus story, the disciples encountered the risen Christ on the road. But that is not where they recognized him. It was not on the road where the mystery was revealed. It was in the breaking of the bread—the Eucharist—where their eyes were opened. At that moment, they finally understood the Scriptures and all the teaching they had received. The same is true today. Jesus, the mystagogue, reveals the mystery to us in the Eucharist. When the catechumens are finally admitted to the Eucharist, it is then that the Holy Spirit will open their minds to understand the Scriptures and the teaching they have received.

Into the Mystery

We enter into mystery by way of symbol and ritual and storytelling. Symbolic expressions give us a glimpse of the larger reality they symbolize. Mystery is revealed to us in the language of symbol.

Think about how this works in love relationships. To express our love, we give flowers, a ring, a promise. We dress up, memorialize anniversaries, make special foods, drink fine wine. We might sing songs or recite poetry. All these symbolic expressions "say" love. In fact, if all we ever did was say the word love without any accompanying symbolic behavior, our feelings might not be clear to our beloved. Our love would not be revealed until it was communicated symbolically.

We know, more or less, the vocabulary of the symbols of human love.

But when it comes to divine love, however, the forms of symbolic expression are not as widely known. When seekers with little religious background come to us, they sometimes find our rituals overwhelming, awe-full, confusing, thrilling, and maybe even frightening. That is because the better our symbols, the more they "say" what they symbolize—the vast, tremendous, awesome mystery of the divine.

Our role as catechumenate ministers is to guide the seekers along the journey of revelation. The guiding that we do is called mystagogy (literally, "to lead one into the mystery"). The one who leads is the mystagogue. The risen Christ, through the power of the Holy Spirit, is always the chief mystagogue. The true revealer of Christ is Christ. The liturgy, where we tell the story of Christ and memorialize the sacrifice of Christ, is the primary place of mystery—the place where the mystery is most fully revealed.

I remember the first time I really understood the idea of the liturgy being a place of mystery in the sense that the fourth-century church fathers talked about it. I grew up going to Mass every day. For my entire childhood, whenever the sisters at my Catholic school would talk about "mystery," I thought they meant something that was too hard to understand. Especially when they talked about the mystery of the Mass, I thought you had to be very holy or very smart to really know what was going on.

When I was a sophomore in college, I went to a liturgy study week at the University of Notre Dame. I thought that maybe if I studied the liturgy, I'd start to unravel the mystery. I signed up for all the workshops and talks. I bought books that the speakers had written. I took lots of notes. And I also went to Mass every day in the chapel because I was used to going to daily Mass at home. I thought it was nice that Mass was available for the conference participants who wanted to get away from all the studying for a little while and just pray.

It was Thursday, I think, when it happened. Just a weekday Mass. Summer Ordinary Time. Maybe thirty people in a worship space that holds one thousand. It was that day my eyes were opened like the disciples on the road to Emmaus. I can't remember any of the workshops I went to or the books I read that week. I threw away my notes. I finally understood that you can't solve the mystery by studying it. You don't have to be holy or smart. You have to be present. What I experienced in that liturgy was the presence of Christ. Not only in the consecrated bread and wine, but in the singing, praying, proclaiming, preaching, moving, sharing, communing, and thanking. Simple gestures, responses, postures—things I'd been doing all my life—suddenly seemed brand-new. I saw for the first time the mystery of Christ.

I had been trying to understand the mystery of Christ through an almost scientific study of holy things. That's a little like trying to understand your spouse by sequencing his or her genome. The Holy Spirit opened my eyes to the fullness of the mystery of Christ through the power of symbol, not science.

> To begin by understanding mystagogy as an eminently christological action means above all to affirm that only the mystery can fully reveal the mystery: mystery reveals itself. This is an essential truth of the Judeo-Christian faith experience: humanity knows God's name because God has freely revealed it. The revelation of the mystery of God is an act that God carries out. (Goffredo Boselli, *The Spiritual Meaning of the Liturgy*, 5)

Studying Scripture and studying doctrine will help strengthen us as disciples. But study alone will never make us into disciples. Study alone is never sufficient to understand the mystery revealed in the liturgy. Revelation is always an act of God because only God can reveal God's self. As mystagogues, we have to lead the seekers to "an appropriate acquaintance with the dogmas and precepts" of the church, but we also have to lead them "to a profound sense of the mystery of salvation" (RCIA 75.1). Doctrine, and even Scripture, are always in service to the fullness of revelation that takes place in the liturgy.

Reading the Bible

The English translation of the Bible that US Catholics read from at Mass is the New American Bible. This is probably the best version for seekers to use for their own reading. Another popular translation that is often used for study in seminaries is the New Revised Standard Version. This is also the version on which the Canadian Lectionary is based. Many "study editions" of these and other translations will provide glossaries, maps, and short dictionaries of biblical terms. Some of the questions that come up when reading the Bible are often answered in footnotes or introductions to the books of the Bible. Many times, the text will offer cross-references to other passages that help make what you are reading clearer or more interesting. It is also enlightening to read a difficult passage in other translations, which you can easily find online.

Word Is Essential

Christians often refer to the "word of God." The phrase itself is symbolic and can reveal several aspects of the one mystery. Our first understanding of the word of God is the "word" God spoke in the beginning and by which all things were made. It is that same "word" (logos) that we speak of on Christmas morning when we proclaim the prologue of John's gospel: "In the beginning was the Word, / and the Word was with God, / and the Word was God" (1:1).

The word of God was also spoken by the Old Testament prophets as a call to righteousness. The Old Testament also personifies the word of God as Wisdom or the Law.

Through the prophet Isaiah, God describes the nature of the word that comes from his mouth:

> It shall not return to me empty,
>   but shall do what pleases me,
>   achieving the end for which I sent it. (Isa 55:11)

(Goffredo Boselli, *The Spiritual Meaning of the Liturgy*, 4)

In the New Testament, the word of God is personified as Jesus himself, who is the continuation in the line of prophets, the perfection of Wisdom, and the completion of the Law. Jesus is the Word of God incarnate.

The word of God is still present in the risen Christ, whose Spirit continues to "speak" through the church. As the church began to speak the word of God, we began to give particular emphasis to the written word. The written word wasn't intended to be history shelved in a library, however. It is a living Word whose fulfillment is proclamation in the midst of the gathered worshiping community.

And over time, the church settled on authoritative texts that we can put our faith in as the true and holy divine word of God. Saint Augustine said, "A man speaks more or less wisely in proportion as he has made more or less progress in the Holy Scriptures" (*De Doctrina Christiana* 4.5).

Even so, it has always been the case that, as essential as the written word is to our faith, Jesus as the Word of God is always most fully present and most fully revealed in the liturgy—first as Logos and then as sacrament.

The Word, as proclaimed in the liturgical assembly, becomes a mystagogical element that reveals God. A third-century catechist named Origen wrote about the first Eucharist:

> It was not the visible bread that he held in his hands which God the Word called his body, but it was the Word in whose sacrament the bread was to be broken. Nor was it the visible drink that he identified as his blood, but it was the Word in whose sacrament the libation was to be poured out. (Boselli, *Spiritual Meaning of the Liturgy*, 12)

In other words, as Catholics, we read Scripture liturgically. The liturgy always interprets Scripture and Scripture interprets liturgy in a unified dynamic. Any reading of Scripture outside of the liturgy always recalls and leads to the mystery of the risen Christ in the liturgy itself.

Liturgy Is Where We Learn and How We Teach

Our takeaway is that in order to effectively teach the core story of Jesus, we catechists have to be imbued with the liturgy. The *Catechism of the Catholic Church* reminds us that the liturgy is the "privileged place for catechizing the People of God" (1074). We are constantly learning and relearning the story ourselves as we become one with Christ in the mystery of the liturgy. There is no substitute for this primary way of knowing Jesus.

> The knowledge offered by the liturgy, therefore, is not entirely intellectual and rational. It is an integral knowledge, an experience that invests all of a person's faculties. In the liturgy, one learns by listening, speaking, seeing, smelling, touching. The senses are the pathway to meaning. (Goffredo Boselli, *The Spiritual Meaning of the Liturgy*, 16)

Likewise, our primary teaching method must be to immerse the seekers in the liturgy. Pope Benedict XVI said "the best catechesis on the Eucharist is the Eucharist itself, celebrated well" (*Sacramentum Caritatis* 64). (In the context of the catechumenate, "Eucharist" should be understood here to refer broadly to the entire celebration of the Mass. Catechumens are "kindly dismissed before the liturgy of the eucharist begins" [RCIA 75.3]. Their celebration of the Liturgy of the Word throughout the liturgical year during the catechumenate and their celebration of the full Eucharist during the period of postbaptismal catechesis or mystagogy will catechize the catechumens-neophytes in the manner described by Pope Benedict.) Our catechesis after the liturgy is mystagogical. It is an extension of the experience of the liturgy itself. Again, from Pope Benedict,

> This basic structure of the Christian experience calls for a process of mystagogy which should always respect three elements:
>
> A. *It interprets the rites in the light of the events of our salvation.* . . .
>
> B. A mystagogical catechesis must also be concerned with *presenting the meaning of the signs* contained in the rites. . . .
>
> C. Finally, a mystagogical catechesis must be concerned with bringing out the *significance of the rites for the Christian life* in all its dimensions—work and responsibility, thoughts and emotions, activity and repose. Part of the mystagogical process is to demonstrate how the mysteries celebrated in the rite are linked to the missionary responsibility of the faithful. (64)

As we go through the rest of the book, examining each of the three major parts of the Jesus story, keep in mind that we are not the primary storytellers. Jesus is the storyteller, and the story unfolds in the celebration of the liturgy.

Tradition

Tradition is the living (Spirit-inspired) memory of Jesus in the Church. Tradition is the lived faith of the People of God. Tradition is the mysterious core, the vivifying center of the Church, the temple of the Holy Spirit. Without this divine presence no one can recognize Jesus as God's self-deed. With this divine presence the recognition of Jesus that is known as faith becomes the skill of the disciple for translating the memory of Jesus into deeds done unto the final consummation of the kingdom of God which remains "not yet." (Michael J. Scanlon, OSA, "Revelation" in *The Modern Catholic Encyclopedia*, 748)

Chapter 4

Field Hospital Protocol:
What to Do First

If, as Pope Francis says, the church is a field hospital after battle, imagine the multitudes of hurting people he sees as he looks over the world. Imagine he then turns to us—the catechists, the teachers, the pastoral leaders—and says, "Go. Heal the wounds." What would we do first?

First Proclamation—Time to Use Our Words

The first thing to do is this: proclaim that Jesus Christ saves us.

Does that make you a little uncomfortable? Catholics aren't used to speaking that way—walking up to people and asking them if they are saved or if they know Jesus is their savior.

But those are the pope's exact words: "The most important thing is the first proclamation: *Jesus Christ has saved you*" (Spadaro, "A Big Heart Open to God," *America*; emphasis added).

What Does "First" Mean?

It is important to understand how the pope is using the word "first."

When I think of my wife, I think of her as my first love. She is not "first" in the sense that she is the first woman I fell in love with. Nor is she "first" in the sense that someday there will be a second or third love, an improved Wife 2.0. She is first in my heart. She is first and foremost.

The first proclamation is not first because there are second and third announcements that will eclipse what came first. It is first in the sense of best or top priority. It is the proclamation that is proclaimed again and again, in every situation, in every age. Every time we proclaim it and every time we hear it, the announcement takes on new and deeper meaning. There isn't some "real catechesis" that we are waiting for. This is it. Here is how the pope says it:

> In catechesis too, we have rediscovered the fundamental role of the first announcement or kerygma, which needs to be the center of all evangelizing activity and all efforts at Church renewal. . . . This first proclamation is called "first" not because it exists at the beginning and can then be forgotten or replaced by other more important things. It is first in a qualitative sense because it is the principal proclamation, the one which we must hear again and again in different ways, the one which we must announce one way or another throughout the process of catechesis, at every level and moment. . . .
>
> We must not think that in catechesis the kerygma gives way to a supposedly more "solid" formation. *Nothing is more solid, profound, secure, meaningful and wisdom-filled than that initial proclamation.* All Christian formation consists of entering more deeply into the kerygma, which is reflected in and constantly illumines the work of catechesis, thereby enabling us to understand more fully the significance of every subject which the latter treats. It is the message capable of responding to the desire for the infinite which abides in every human heart. (Joy of the Gospel, 164, 165; emphasis added)

It seems simple enough, and yet, for many of us, the story of Jesus is a stumbling block. We try to make it too complicated. We think we don't know enough. We worry we will offend others. We don't know where to start. We don't know where to end.

Let's make it really simple. There are three big parts to the story that you have to remember:

1. The beginning

2. The climax

3. The end

Each of those three parts has three subparts, for a total of nine pieces of the story.

In order to tell the story effectively, we have to prepare ourselves before we can teach the story.

Have Faith

First and most important, we have to have faith. We have to have faith in Jesus and faith in the gifts that we have been given.

The model of faith for us is Abraham. Abraham believed, in spite of what looked like insurmountable obstacles, that God would make him the father of a great nation. This is such an important point for us and for our seekers. Faith seldom makes sense in a logical way.

Saint Paul explains this in his Letter to the Romans (see Rom 4). He says that if you work hard and get paid for your work, you would never refer to your paycheck as a gift. You earned it. But what if the job was too big for you? What if the only way you could do the job was if God did it for you? What if the only way you could do the thing you were trying to do was to give up doing it and trust God to do it for you? That trust in God, in spite of the job being unimaginably big, is faith.

The Letter to the Hebrews says, "Faith is the realization of what is hoped for and evidence of things not seen" (11:1). Our seekers have entered "the way of faith" (RCIA 1). Our job, as guides on that journey, is to provide example through our own "assurance of things hoped for." We have to have the conviction of heart that "things not seen" are true and reliable because God gave us a promise—just as God gave a promise to Abraham.

My Abraham moment

I sometimes think of my move to California as an "Abraham moment." Like Abraham, I was called to move to a "foreign land." I left my Midwestern roots, my family and friends, everything I knew. I moved two thousand miles from home. That is about five hundred miles more than the distance between London and Moscow.

You have to cross two mountain ranges to get from the Midwestern United States to California. These days, with air and train travel and even car travel, the trip isn't the arduous journey it was when California first became part of the US. But it is still a long distance culturally from much of the rest of the country. It took me a very long time to feel like I "spoke the language" here. It took me a long time to feel at home.

However, without getting overly dramatic about it, I felt like I was on a mission (I still do). I felt like I had been called and sent. And I prayed daily for the faith to accept my call and try to live up to it as best as I could. In Joy of the Gospel, Pope Francis said,

> I dream of a "missionary option," that is, a missionary impulse capable of transforming everything, so that the Church's customs, ways of doing things, times and schedules, language and structures can be suitably channeled for the evangelization of today's world rather than for her self-preservation. (27)

I think the missionary option applies not only to institutions, but to ourselves as well. When I moved to California, I had to let go of my customs, ways of doing things, schedules, structures, even some of my language. It was a big leap of faith. We ask the seekers to make a similar kind of leap.

Living a Christian life is hard work. By claiming our Christian faith, we automatically set ourselves against the daunting forces of the world that promote selfishness. Pope Francis says, "Our faith is challenged to discern how wine can come from water and how wheat can grow in the midst of weeds" (Joy of the Gospel, 84).

Our challenge in faith is to always remain joyful, even in the face of discouragement. The pope famously said there is no place in the church for sourpusses:

> One of the more serious temptations which stifles boldness and zeal is a defeatism which turns us into querulous and disillusioned pessimists, "sourpusses." Nobody can go off to battle unless he is fully convinced of victory beforehand. If we start without confidence, we have already lost half the battle and we bury our talents. While painfully aware of our own frailties, we have to march on without giving in, keeping in mind what the Lord said to Saint Paul: "My grace is sufficient for you, for my power is made perfect in weakness" (2 Cor 12:9). (Joy of the Gospel, 85)

Evangelize

Next, we have to make evangelization our top priority. The church exists to evangelize, and we are baptized to go out and share the Good News. Pope Francis says,

> Being Church means . . . that we are to be God's leaven in the midst of humanity. It means proclaiming and bringing God's salvation into our world, which often goes astray and needs to be encouraged, given hope and strengthened on the way. The Church must be a place of mercy freely given, where everyone can feel welcomed, loved, forgiven and encouraged to live the good life of the Gospel. (Joy of the Gospel, 114)

As Catholics, we are not known for our evangelization skills. We tend to be quiet about our faith, careful not to offend or make others feel awkward. We absolutely love the meme, "Preach the gospel at all times, and when necessary, use words." That notion seemingly lets us off the hook about talking about our faith. Can't we just live by example and let that serve as our evangelization?

Pope Francis says over and over again, Go forth! For Francis, there is only one image of the church that is life-giving—a church that goes forth, that goes out of itself, into the streets, to proclaim good news. The pope wants us to be a church that goes to the peripheries.

This is a crucial point for RCIA teams. Too often, we stay inside the church and wait for someone to knock on the door. But Pope Francis says that when we do that, we might actually be keeping Jesus inside the church:

> In Revelation, Jesus says that he is at the door and knocks. Obviously, the text refers to his knocking from the outside in order to enter, but I think about the times in which Jesus knocks from within so that we will let him come out. (Pre-conclave address to the General Congregation meetings of the cardinals; quoted in Cindy Wooden, "Pope Francis' Constant Refrain," *Catholic News Service*)

Evangelization truly is the pope's constant refrain: "Jesus does not tell the Apostles or us to form an exclusive group, a group of the *elite*. Jesus says: go out and make disciples of all people" (Pope Francis, General Audience, June 12, 2013). Francis is not the first pope to speak this way. Here are some other examples:

- "The Church is missionary by nature and her principal task is evangelization" (Pope Benedict XVI, Address to International Congress of Military Ordinariates, October 26, 2006).

- "No believer in Christ, no institution of the Church can avoid this supreme duty: to proclaim Christ to all peoples" (Pope John Paul II, *Redemptoris Missio*, December 7, 1990).

- The Church "exists in order to evangelize" (Pope Paul VI, *Evangelii Nuntiandi*, December 8, 1975).

Whenever I hear that Catholics are supposed to evangelize, I think of the street preacher who is usually around on weekend nights in my city's downtown. He stands on a small stepladder and shouts into a portable loudspeaker. He quotes Scripture and explains to passersby why they are going to burn in hell if they don't accept Jesus as their personal savior.

Well, I'm never going to evangelize that way, and I don't believe that's what the popes are asking us to do. But how are Catholics supposed to evangelize? How do we let Jesus out? Where are the peripheries? How do we get there?

The peripheries are those places where people are marginalized and forgotten. They are the places where people lack hope and joy. Pope Francis said,

> Each one of us can think of persons who live without hope and are immersed in a profound sadness that they try to escape by thinking they can find happiness in alcohol, drugs, gambling, the power of money, promiscuity. . . . We who have the joy of knowing that we are not orphans, that we have a father, cannot be indifferent to those yearning for love and for hope. With your witness, with your smile, you need to let others know that the same Father loves them, too. (Wooden, "Pope Francis' Constant Refrain")

That last line is important. It is what we need to teach the seekers. It is not just our witness that is important. Along with our witness, we have to let those who are without hope know that the Father who loves us also loves them. The promise that God made to Abraham and the promise God made to us is the same promise God makes to people who are hopeless, sad, and joyless. We have to say that.

Go Out to the Poor

Notice that the examples Pope Francis consistently uses when he talks about going forth are focused on the poor and the outcast. The wealthy are certainly in need of evangelization. But it is the poor, first of all, who need to hear good news:

If the whole Church takes up this missionary impulse, she has to go forth to everyone without exception. But to whom should she go first? When we read the Gospel we find a clear indication: not so much our friends and wealthy neighbors, but above all the poor and the sick, those who are usually despised and overlooked, "those who cannot repay you" (Lk 14:14). There can be no room for doubt or for explanations which weaken so clear a message. Today and always, "the poor are the privileged recipients of the Gospel." (Joy of the Gospel, 48)

When we think of the poor, we often think of those who lack material resources. Physical poverty is usually obvious because it includes lack of things such as those Jesus listed in the Last Judgment story—food, water, shelter, clothing, medicine. However, there are several types of poverty.

Other kinds of poverty are sometimes harder to see. Cultural poverty includes things like illiteracy, reduced chances for education, slim job prospects, and racial, religious, or sexual discrimination that excludes groups of people from social and cultural life.

Another kind of poverty is loneliness. Someone might be lonely after losing a loved one. Or a mental or physical disability inhibits a person from making relationships. Discrimination also plays a role in this type of poverty.

And then there is spiritual poverty. People who are in this kind of poverty lack hope. They see little meaning in life and find no joy.

All of these forms of poverty feed off of each other and cause complex layers of problems that demand a multipronged approach to bring a merciful response. If someone doesn't have food, we have to provide food, immediately. But why doesn't this person have food? Perhaps he or she can't get a job because of lack of education. Or perhaps he or she suffers from a mental illness, possibly following the sudden death of a loved one.

Pope Francis's mandate to go forth is not confined to only the material forms of poverty. Think of people in your own life—in your workplace or your neighborhood—who might be trapped in one of these forms of poverty. How might you "go forth" to them? What would someone in poverty need to see in you or hear from you to experience the Good News?

Three to Get Ready . . .

So our three-step preparation process for teaching the core of the faith is this:

1. Have faith and remain joyful in that faith.

2. Make telling the story of Jesus (evangelization) our number-one priority.

3. Go forth to tell the story first of all and always to the poor.

In the next chapter, we'll discuss some practical planning steps for teaching the core of our faith.

Chapter 5

Making a Plan

The core of our faith is the story of Jesus. That story can be grouped into three parts and each part has three subparts:

1. The beginning: Know who God is
   A. The most important lesson seekers must learn
   B. God became one of us
   C. What Jesus did and why it matters

2. The climax: Jesus makes a difference
   A. The Jesus sacrifice
   B. The resurrection
   C. The Jesus offer

3. The end: Walking the talk
   A. Everybody matters
   B. The secret to discipleship
   C. Announce the Good News

This story is the story of Jesus. When we tell it, we are evangelizing—literally telling the "Good News." There are many reasons not to evangelize. It's not socially acceptable to talk about religion. It's embarrassing. We don't know what to say. We don't know enough theology. We don't have enough training.

Pope Francis says we cannot let these roadblocks stop us. The need is too great. The crisis is too profound. The mission is too urgent. He recalls the story of the Samaritan woman who became an evangelizer after speaking with Jesus for only a few moments. The pope asks, if she can do it, what are we waiting for?

> Every Christian is challenged, here and now, to be actively engaged in evangelization; indeed, anyone who has truly experienced God's saving love does not need much time or lengthy training to go out and proclaim that love. (Joy of the Gospel, 120)

God is madly in love with us. Anyone who has experienced that love is qualified—is required—to go tell others that God is also madly in love with them.

We Are All Missionary Disciples

The mandate to tell others about God's love is the mission that Jesus gave to the church. When we, like the Samaritan woman, tell others about Jesus and about God's love for the world, we are fulfilling the mission. We are being missionaries. When I was a child, the sisters who taught in my school would take up collections and ask us to pray for the missionaries. I thought of missionaries as nuns and priests in faraway countries. However, Pope Francis says that all of the baptized are called to be missionary disciples.

I'm not sure what those nuns and priests were doing in those other countries. The sisters were not very clear on that. So as I got older and it started to dawn on me that I was also supposed to be a missionary, I didn't have a very clear model of what to do. Then, in 1997, the Congregation for the Clergy issued the *General Directory for Catechesis* (GDC), which says,

> [The] mission *ad gentes*, regardless of the zone or context in which it is realized, is the missionary responsibility most specifically entrusted to the Church by Jesus and thus the exemplary

model for all her missionary activity. New evangelization cannot supplant or be substituted for "the mission *ad gentes*," which continues to be the paradigm and primary task of missionary activity.

"The model for all catechesis is the baptismal catechumenate when, by specific formation, an adult converted to belief is brought to explicit profession of baptismal faith during the Paschal Vigil." This catechumenal formation should inspire the other forms of catechesis in both their objectives and in their dynamism. . . .

In this way catechesis, situated in the context of the Church's mission of evangelization and seen as an essential moment of that mission, receives from evangelization a missionary dynamic which deeply enriches it and defines its own identity. The ministry of catechesis appears, then, as a fundamental ecclesial service for the realization of the missionary mandate of Jesus. (GDC 59)

That's a lot of "church speak," but once I understood it, a light clicked on for me. The mission *ad gentes* is literally the mission "to the nations"—that is, to all the people in the world who do not know Jesus. That mission is the "primary task" of the church.

The model for all catechesis is the "baptismal catechumenate." Instead of "baptismal catechumenate," we often say "RCIA." They can mean the same thing, but we have to be sure we know what we mean by "RCIA." The baptismal catechumenate is a process by which those who have no faith are "converted to belief." Often we have people in our RCIA processes who already believe in Jesus. So that is not what the GDC means by the "baptismal catechumenate." The GDC means the formation process by which someone is brought from unbelief to belief and then baptized into Christ.

When we are engaged in that conversion process, the GDC says that we are fundamentally serving and realizing the mission that Jesus gave to the church. In other words, the catechumenate is the model for our work as missionary disciples. That was the light that clicked on for me.

So when we set out to make a parish plan for mission, the catechumenate is our template for the plan.

The catechumenate is not the plan (except for the catechumens). Rather, it should inspire us and guide us as we develop our parish pastoral plans. The GDC lists five ways the catechumenate inspires the larger parish mission, *ad gentes*. I have rewritten them to make the language more conversational. You can read the original text from the *General Directory for Catechesis* at paragraph 91. Here is my version:

1. The catechumenate serves as a constant reminder to the whole parish of the vital importance of initiating new people into the community. The essential components of initiation are catechesis and the celebration of the initiation sacraments—baptism, confirmation, and Eucharist.

2. The catechumenate is the responsibility of every member of the parish. This is a radical decentralization of the missionary activity of the church and requires every Christian to think of himself or herself as an equal partner in the work Jesus left us.

3. The catechumenate is steeped in the mystery of Christ's death and resurrection. Therefore everyone involved in the work of initiation must work hard to clearly reveal the paschal nature of our faith. The Easter Vigil is the source and inspiration for all catechesis.

4. The catechumenate is also an initial starting point for inculturation. The Son of God became human in a concrete place and time in history. That is to say, Jesus had a culture. Therefore, we accept and celebrate the cultures of all those who seek to join us. Different cultures hear the word of God in different ways, and it is our job to find ways of incorporating all those different styles of hearing into the catholicity of the church.

5. Finally, we understand the catechumenate to be *"a process of formation"* (GDC 91). The catechumenate is not a textbook to be gotten through nor a series of meetings to attend nor a required number of service projects. It is a comprehensive formation, gradually accomplished in definite stages. It is marked and celebrated in "meaningful rites, symbols, biblical

and liturgical signs" (GDC 91). Most of all, it is a formation handed on by us, the Christian faithful, the Body of Christ.

So how would you take these five inspirations and create a plan for announcing the first proclamation? Here are five steps (inspired by Bill Huebsch's "Parish Pastoral Planning Guide to Prepare for the Jubilee Year of Mercy").

Step 1—Understand What Pope Francis Is Asking of Us

Pope Francis has set out a comprehensive agenda for the church in Joy of the Gospel. His exhortation that we have to make the first proclamation over and over again—"Jesus Christ loves you; he gave his life to save you; and now he is living at your side every day to enlighten, strengthen and free you"—is the foundation of our pastoral planning. Spend one to three meetings with your planning team reading and discussing this bedrock document. Schedule more meetings if necessary. Do not move forward until the planning team has a solid understanding of the pope's message.

Step 2—Practice Talking

Joy of the Gospel has an introduction and five chapters. Schedule one to three meetings to practice summary statements about each section. Say these out loud to each other. Work to make your message simple and clear. Use language and phrases that all the different age groups and ethnic groups in your parish would understand. Can you explain chapter 1 to the First Communion candidates? Can you explain chapter 2 to a new immigrant from Mexico? Can you explain chapter 3 to a couple preparing for marriage? Practice with each other, and give honest feedback.

Step 3—Review the Parish Bulletin and Calendar

Schedule one to three meetings to audit every activity and meeting that takes place in your parish. Engage in frank and honest discussion about how effectively each activity makes the first proclamation—"Jesus Christ loves you; he gave his life to save you; and now he is living at your side every day to enlighten, strengthen and free you."

Step 4—Get Practical

Based on your review of current parish activities, schedule one to three meetings to brainstorm what to stop doing and what to continue or start doing. Name key players in the parish who can help you with the development of new initiatives. Talk honestly about the implications for your parish budget.

Step 5—Write It Down

Schedule one to three meetings to sum everything up. Check your summary against the text of Joy of the Gospel to make sure you are on track. Write down priorities. Write down next steps. Add goals to your parish and individual calendars. Develop an initial budget. Choose a date for a parish-wide meeting to begin a dialogue with the whole community on how to answer Pope Francis's challenge: "Heal the wounds, heal the wounds."

Who Are We Talking To?

For our plan to be effective, we have to know who we will be talking to. Broadly speaking, there are three levels of seekers that we encounter. We have to shape our first proclamation to fit each type. In order of urgency, the three are

1. unbelievers and those indifferent to the faith;

2. inquirers and catechumens who are not yet true believers;

3. believers in need of constant renewal.

1. Unbelievers

Those who don't believe or are indifferent to the faith are our first priority. Their wounds are the most serious. When we want to communicate God's saving love to unbelievers, we have to start with the "silent witness" of the way we live. Pope Francis says that there are four behaviors by which Christians will be known:

1. Love

2. Harmony

3. Joy

4. Suffering (See Address to Participants in the Plenary of the Pontifical Council for Promoting New Evangelization, October 14, 2013.)

These four ways of living give evidence of our faith and give evidence to the world about what we believe. It is by living according to these principles that unbelievers will begin to see what it is to live in freedom and joy.

If we live this way, we will become curiosities for others. Our behavior will seem odd. It will raise questions. Pope Francis says that living as Christians through love, harmony, joy, and suffering gives rise to questions:

- "Why do they live that way?"

- "What urges them on?" (See Address to Pontifical Council for Promoting New Evangelization, October 14, 2013.)

When unbelievers become curious about our lives, we have the opportunity to bolster our "silent witness" with an "explicit witness." As the unbelievers begin to notice us and ask us questions, we can invite them to explore a relationship with Jesus.

2. Inquirers and Catechumens

When curiosity results in a genuine desire to know more, unbelievers become inquirers and eventually catechumens. (The term "inquirers" is also sometimes used to refer to Christians of other denominations who wish to become Catholic. We also call these folks "candidates." Depending upon their individual faith journeys, these seekers might be either inquirers or believers.)

Inquirers and catechumens are our second priority. They have started to heal. We think of inquirers and catechumens as having a spark of faith, but not yet a grounded, solid faith. When we start to see signs of healing and conversion in the hearts of the inquirers, we can begin a deeper conversation about the first proclamation. Some signs of conversion we might look for in the inquirers include

- an initial conversion;
- a desire to change their lives;
- a desire to enter into a relationship with God in Christ;
- signs of the first stirrings of repentance;
- a start to the practice of calling upon God in prayer;
- a sense of the church;
- some experience of the company and spirit of Christian community (see RCIA 42).

Once inquirers are really ready to go deeper and become catechumens, we can develop the first proclamation through four key lenses:

1. How do Christians hear and obey the living word of God?
2. How do Christians experience Jesus living beside us every day?
3. How do Christians express their joy, especially through praise and worship of God?
4. How do Christians extend Jesus's mission of mercy into the world? (See RCIA 75.)

3. Believers

True believers are those who have committed to live as disciples of Jesus according to the four disciplines listed above. Believers can still suffer from their wounds, but they have been saved from death. They have been healed.

As disciples, we are continually going deeper into the first proc-lamation. We never cease exploring the depths of its meaning for us. Imagine you are Mary at the tomb. You are bereft. You don't know how you can go on. And then Jesus says your name. Your name. At that moment, you recognize him. You are instantly freed from your desolation. You know him, and he knows you. You are so overjoyed, you run to tell the others. You run to tell the whole world.

Would you ever tire of that? Would you ever run out of things to say? Would you ever leave that life-changing event behind for some supposedly more solid form of Christian formation? Of course not. It would define your entire life as a disciple.

To reemphasize, those most in need of experiencing the fresh-ness and fragrance of the Gospel are people who are not in our churches. They are not asking to become Catholic, and they are not in our RCIA processes. The people who are bleeding out and need tourniquets are outside the walls of our churches; they are on the peripheries. Our parishes and our RCIA teams will have to explore new ways of getting outside the walls of the church and out into the places most in need of healing. This is truly what it means to be a field hospital church.

At the end of each of the following sections that deal with the nine parts of the first proclamation, you will see a box titled "Train-ing in Christian Life." You will find there three suggested ways to focus on the first proclamation. Each suggestion is geared toward one of the levels of seekers we discussed above.

Primary proclamation is the type of activity we would do to prepare ourselves to make the first proclamation to unbelievers or those indifferent to the faith.

Initiatory catechesis is the type of activity we would do to tell the story of Jesus to catechumens and other inquirers who have begun to have irresistible questions about the way Christians live and why we live the way we do.

Ongoing catechesis is the type of activity we would do to delve deeper into the first proclamation with believers and members of the faithful.

These brief examples are meant to be idea-starters. You can and will think of many other ways to tell the story of Jesus to the world.

Let's turn now to the first part of the story of Jesus that we have to tell.

Chapter 6

The Beginning: Know Who God Is

The Most Important Lesson Seekers Must Learn

God is madly in love with us. That is the most important lesson seekers have to learn. Indeed, it is the most important lesson we all have to learn.

This is crucial. A 2008 survey by the Pew Research Center reported that 25 percent of US adults believe that "God is an impersonal force" (Benjamin Wormald, *U.S. Religious Landscape Survey*). What this means is that one-quarter of the seekers in your initiation process probably don't believe that God loves them or even that God can love them. For them, God is not a person and is not someone capable of a personal, loving relationship.

Of those seekers who do believe that God is a personal God, capable of loving us, they perhaps believe that God chooses not to love them—because they are unworthy or insignificant.

Our First Task

Whatever the case, our first job is to proclaim the good news that God loves each person, exactly as he or she is, unconditionally.

> "God is love, and he who abides in love abides in God, and
> God abides in him" (1 Jn 4:16). These words from the First
> Letter of John express with remarkable clarity the heart of
> the Christian faith: the Christian image of God and the re-
> sulting image of mankind and its destiny. In the same verse,
> Saint John also offers a kind of summary of the Christian
> life: "We have come to know and to believe in the love God
> has for us." (Pope Benedict XVI, *Deus Caritas Est* 1)

The multiple stories of God's interaction with humans show us
that this is true. The very act of creation is an act of love. God freely
chose, for no reason, to create. And the climax of that creation is
us—made in the very image and likeness of God. God created us
as partners, as people capable of love, so that God could love us
and we could love God.

To make us capable of love, real love as God loves, means we
have to have free will. In other words, we have to be able to choose
to love or to reject love. And reject we did, over and over again in
the stories of the Old Testament. In each and every case, God stays
true to us, turning toward us with care, even when we rejected God.

Humanity's Fall

You can recall many of these stories yourself: the disobedience
of Adam and Eve; the murder of Abel by his brother Cain; the
corruption of society that caused the great Flood; the tower of
Babel; the worship of the golden calf by the Israelites. There are,
of course, many more stories about how humanity rejected God,
culminating with Jesus's crucifixion.

In each and every case, God did not abandon us, but was instead merciful with us. The point of all these stories is not to give
us a history lesson. It is to remind us that God always chooses to
love us. God's very being is defined by mercy.

When we talk about God as divine, we mean that God is irrationally loving and merciful. When we talk about being made in God's image and likeness, we mean that we are being who God made us to be when we are irrationally loving and merciful.

Saving grace

On October 2, 2006, thirty-two-year-old Charles Carl Roberts IV walked into an Amish schoolhouse in Nickel Mines, Pennsylvania, and slashed a long, wide swath of darkness across the gentle community. After releasing the boys and adults, he threatened to kill the ten remaining girls. The girls responded by asking him to pray with them.

When he refused, thirteen-year-old Marian Fisher stepped up to him and said, "Shoot me and leave the other ones loose." The madman then began shooting the girls, killing five and severely wounding the others ("Amish bury 5th Victim," *Associated Press*).

The grandfather of two sisters killed told an interviewer he bore no anger toward the killer's family. And he had forgiven the killer. "How is that possible?" asked the reporter. "Through God's help," replied the grandfather (Ann Curry, "Amish Display the True Meaning of Forgiveness," *NBC News*).

After shooting the girls, Roberts killed himself. There were seventy-five mourners at his funeral. Thirty of them were Amish. The Amish received over a million dollars in donations since the shootings. They pledged some of it to help Roberts's wife and his three children.

The Catechism says grace *"escapes our experience* and cannot be known except by faith" (2005). Perhaps it can also be known in the examples of grace we see, examples such as the Amish give us. Examples of unlimited, uncontainable, unrelenting, almost unbelievable grace.

Start with Your Story

When we are teaching seekers about who God is—a God who, as we know from Scripture, loves them no matter what—we can tell them these stories from the Bible. But that is probably not where we should start. We should start by telling our own stories.

When you encounter seekers, oftentimes they are looking for a change. But change is difficult. Did you know most people who survive a heart attack do not change their lifestyle and eating habits? People are very resistant to change. However, when you tell your story of change—your story of dying and rising—your chances of helping seekers to make a true change in their lives rise dramatically.

When did God love you for no reason? When did God forgive you when you totally didn't deserve it? When did God heal you from a wound you thought was irreparable? When did God rescue you from a place so dark that you didn't know light existed? These are the elements of your story that will stir up irresistible questions in the hearts of the seekers. When you talk about these actions of God in your life, seekers will want to know more.

When we ask seekers to believe in God, we are asking them to believe in a God who saves. We tell our stories of when God saved us, and we share the promise that God will do the same for the seekers. Our first proof that God loves the seekers is that God loves us—no matter what. And next, our proof is the multitude of ways God has loved humanity throughout history.

And the ultimate proof that God loves us is that God became one of us. That's what we are going to look at in the next lesson.

How do we tell our dying and rising stories?
Remember these points:

- The goal is not to make people listen but to create curiosity.

- Good stories are about people.

- Good stories stir up emotions.

- Good stories don't tell; they show.

Five steps to telling a great paschal mystery story:

1. Remember a significant dying and rising moment.

2. Recall the details, the people, the actions, the feeling.

3. Reflect on what it meant; what it connected/revealed for you; what it reminded you of.

4. Name how you were changed.

5. Name why that story gives you hope in Christ.

Use storytelling to influence conversion:

- Listen first to the story of the seeker; ask good questions; be patient.

- Don't listen for logic; listen for understanding.

- Listen to learn, not to reinforce what you know.

- Cast the seeker as the "hero" in your story.

- Instead of trying to convince people you're right, just tell a story.

- Use your story to overcome negative emotions.

Training in Christian Life

Primary proclamation

Spend some time journaling about your own story. Write a page or so on each of these questions: When did God love you for no reason? When did God forgive you when you totally didn't deserve it? When did God heal you from a wound you thought was irreparable? When did God rescue you from a place so dark that you didn't know light existed? Imagine how you might talk about these experiences in "ordinary language" that might make sense to someone who doesn't believe in God.

Initiatory catechesis

Meet one-on-one with each seeker (or set up one-on-ones with each seeker and a team member). Listen to the seeker's story. Don't talk much; just listen. When the seeker is finished, make two connections: one to your own story of faith and one to the faith story of a saint or spiritual hero.

Ongoing catechesis

Read the story of Cesar Chavez in the *United States Catholic Catechism for Adults* (323–24). Discuss how we sometimes fail each other as human beings and how God is always with us, no matter how bleak our conditions may seem.

God Became One of Us

In his announcement of the jubilee year of mercy, Pope Francis gives us the whole reason for God becoming one of us:

Jesus Christ is the face of the Father's mercy. These words might well sum up the mystery of the Christian faith. (The Face of Mercy, 1)

The Mystery of Christian Faith

We have faith because Jesus is the face of God's mercy. That seems obvious. But let's look deeper. When Christians say that we know that Jesus is God (or the face of God's mercy), we can sometimes presume that's true because we know who God is.

In other words, we think that because we know what we mean by "God," we know that Jesus fits the definition of "God." But, in fact, the reverse is true. It is only because we know who Jesus is that we can know what "God" means.

The *Catechism of the Catholic Church* says that we should never "confuse our image of God—'the inexpressible, the incomprehensible, the invisible, the ungraspable'—with our human representations. Our human words always fall short of the mystery of God" (42).

Philip, Jesus's disciple, could not quite wrap his head around this. After following Jesus for a long time, eating with him, listening to his teachings, seeing his mighty acts, Philip asked Jesus to "show us the Father, and that will be enough for us" (John 14:8).

I could have said that line. I have said that line. I am always looking for more proof when it comes to faith. And every time I say something like that, I am sure Jesus sighs and perhaps smacks his forehead. He said to Philip,

> Have I been with you for so long a time and you still do not know me, Philip? Whoever has seen me has seen the Father. How can you say, "Show us the Father?" Do you not believe that I am in the Father and the Father is in me? (John 14:9-10)

If we have seen Jesus, we have seen God. And Jesus is mystery. We are pretty comfortable saying the risen Christ is mystery. We have to remember that the historical Jesus, before the resurrection, is also mystery—in the same way all humans are mystery. The mystery of Christian faith that Pope Francis mentions is founded on the person of Jesus Christ—the person who showed us the mystery of God.

The Culmination of Revelation

The next thing the pope says in that announcement is,

> Mercy has become living and visible in Jesus of Nazareth, reaching its culmination in him. (The Face of Mercy, 1)

The pope then goes on to list a whole bunch of ways God had been revealing God's self throughout the Old Testament. God had been making himself known to us for a very long time. And at the right time (the "fullness of time" [Gal 4:4]), he sent Jesus to us

> . . . to reveal his love for us in a definitive way. Whoever sees Jesus sees the Father (cf. John 14:9). Jesus of Nazareth, by his words, his actions, and his entire person reveals the mercy of God. (1)

God Is What Jesus Does

An important understanding for ourselves and for the seekers is that Jesus didn't so much tell us about God as much as he showed us who God is. That is what Pope Francis means when he says that Jesus is the "face of the Father's mercy."

We know the story of Jesus because of the four gospels. Did you ever wonder why we have four gospels? There is only one Jesus and one story, so why four gospels? Well, if Jesus is mystery, words will fail us when we try to define or explain that mystery. The gospel writers are not trying to create definitive biographies of Jesus that simply recount the facts of his life. Each of the four gospels tells stories about what Jesus did, but they emphasize different stories for different reasons. This is also part of the human mystery. No two people will tell the same stories about you in the same way.

Mark focuses on mystery and paradox. Some people say that in Mark's account, we most clearly see the human, vulnerable side of Jesus. And at the same time, Mark emphasizes the divine power of the Son. Oddly, Jesus is always telling people who witness his miracles to keep quiet about them. But then he goes on to perform more powerful miracles. The true nature of Jesus's identity is revealed on the cross when the centurion recognizes who Jesus is and professes, "Truly this man was the Son of God!" (15:39). Mark was writing to people who, like Jesus, sometimes feel abandoned and weak. The vulnerable yet powerful Jesus of Mark's gospel still speaks to people today who suffer and lack hope.

Matthew wrote about Jesus as a teacher and guide. In Mathew's gospel, there are clear parallels of Jesus's ministry and that of Moses. Jesus is identified both as Son of David and Son of Abraham. The flight to Egypt is only recorded in Matthew, and it is a reminder of Moses leading the Israelites out of Egypt in the great exodus. Jesus's teaching is presented in five discourses, which echo the five books of the Pentateuch of Moses. Salvation comes through faithfulness to Jesus's teachings, which are summarized in the Beatitudes, which are themselves an echo of Moses delivering the Ten Commandments. People seeking a clear path for living a life of faith will be especially drawn to this gospel.

Luke did not only write a gospel; he also wrote the Acts of the Apostles. Even though they are presented separately in the Bible, they are really two parts of one work. In the gospel (part 1), Luke establishes Jesus's life and ministry as the model for the church. In Acts (part 2), the church imitates the life and ministry of Jesus. Luke's work has often been called the "social justice gospel." For Luke in particular, Jesus's tender care for the poor, the outcast, the sinner, and the afflicted is the template for the action of the church. It is Luke who has Mary sing,

> He has shown might with his arm,
>> dispersed the arrogant of mind and heart.
> He has thrown down the rulers from their thrones
>> but lifted up the lowly.
> The hungry he has filled with good things;
>> the rich he has sent away empty. (1:51-53)

Luke emphasizes the mercy and compassion of Jesus, the role of the Spirit in the life of the church, the importance of prayer, and Jesus's concern for women.

John's gospel is structured differently than the previous three. John makes clear that Jesus is fully human (the Word made "flesh," 1:14) while also describing Jesus in very exalted language that emphasizes his divinity. John combines the everyday (bread, vine, light, sheep gate) with the mystical (Mary as Eve, the Beloved Disciple as intimate friend, Mary of Magdala as yearning seeker). Every Christmas morning, John reminds us that Jesus is Incarnate Word (Logos), who has been with us since the beginning of time (see John 1:1-18). John's account of Jesus's life includes stories of powerful miracles that do not appear in the other gospels. These miracles are signs of Jesus's authority, which comes from the Father ("The words that I speak to you I do not speak on my own. The Father who dwells in me is doing his works" [14:10]). One of the main points of John's gospel was to bolster the faith of John's followers that Jesus is Messiah. That is also a message we need to reemphasize today.

The gospel writers could focus on these different aspects of Jesus because of how he lived and what their communities witnessed when he was among them. If we add in the rest of the New Testament writers, we find even more characterizations of Jesus that reflect different understandings of who he is. This diversity of "Christs" is a good thing because it allows the church to speak to many different people in their individual situations. The *Rite of Christian Initiation of Adults* says that the spiritual journey of adults varies according to the particular circumstances of each person (see RCIA 5). One of the ways we can help guide the seekers on the way of faith is to help them connect with the "Jesus" that most speaks to their hearts.

The thing that is constant in all the writings about Jesus is that he was human, lived as a human, struggled with human foibles, and is in full solidarity with all of humanity. And yet, he is also the full revelation of God—so much so that he is truly God, while at the same time truly human. The bishops at the Second Vatican Council said that Jesus is "the most intimate truth which this revelation gives us about God and the salvation of man shines forth in Christ, who is himself both the mediator and the sum total of Revelation" (Constitution on Divine Revelation, 2).

The New Testament writers knew who Jesus was because of what he did—his miracles and signs, his teaching, and his deep compassion for the poor. Most powerfully, they knew who Jesus was because of the resurrection. And they also knew who Jesus was because of what each of them was looking for and what Jesus did for each of them personally.

In a similar way, the story you tell about Jesus is going to be influenced by your own life—what you are looking for and what Jesus has done for you.

Jesus told Philip, "Whoever has seen me has seen the Father." And we could add, whoever has seen you has seen Jesus. The story you tell, mostly by the way you live and the things you do, will "sum up the mystery of the Christian faith" for the seekers you encounter.

Seeing Jesus Today

The gospel stories of Jesus give us a template for recognizing Jesus today. Our experience of Jesus is more like the community in the Acts of the Apostles than that of the communities in the gospels. That is, we know who Jesus is because the church is living in the glory of the resurrected Christ. Like the early church, we reflect on the stories of Jesus and pattern our lives on those stories. We do this in many ways. The way we forgive and offer mercy in our families, the way we reach out to and care for the poor, and the way we live together in Christian community. We see Jesus most clearly in the way we pray and worship, especially Sunday Eucharist. We do all of these things because they are the things the first disciples did after the resurrection. It was by living in this way that the first disciples remained faithful to Jesus's instruction to "do this in memory of me."

In the next section, we will look more closely at what Jesus did that showed the first disciples, and us, who God is.

Is there a biography of Jesus?

The Gospels, of course, did not pretend to be historical documents. While they do contain fragments of history, their principal intent is to bring their readers to faith. So no full historical portrait of Jesus of Nazareth is possible, or at least none completely satisfying to the Western contemporary mind. This quest of the historical Jesus has continued, off and on, from the 1770s down to the present time. . . . Jesus of Nazareth has emerged as a wandering preacher and teacher who also had powers as a healer. But what remains clear in the quest is that the historical Jesus that we perceive dimly through the fragments of history comes alive to us only in faith. (Robert J. Schreiter, CPPS, "Jesus Christ— Pastoral-Liturgical Tradition," in *The Collegeville Pastoral Dictionary of Biblical Theology*)

Training in Christian Life

Primary proclamation

Write a spiritual biography of Jesus based on your experience of faith. How has the person of Jesus Christ been present to you throughout your faith journey? How would you describe that faith journey to unbelievers?

Initiatory catechesis

Share with the seekers that the name "Jesus" means "God saves" and that "Christ" means "anointed one." Ask them to tell you a story about when they were saved (or needed to be saved) from something. Ask them to tell you about a time they were chosen ("anointed") for an important task.

Ongoing catechesis

Read paragraph 8 of Pope Francis's letter The Face of Mercy. Discuss how Jesus is part of the Holy Trinity and how we experience the love of the Trinity through him. Discuss the pope's episcopal motto (which he quotes at the end of paragraph 8): "*miserando atque eligendo*," which means "because he saw him through the eyes of mercy and chose him." It is a reference to Jesus calling Matthew to be a disciple, even though Matthew was a sinner. How does Jesus's merciful choice of Matthew (and us) reveal both Jesus's humanity and his divinity?

What Jesus Did and Why It Matters

What we do in catechumenate ministry is teach people what they need to know to become Catholic and to live as Christians. But why do we do that? Why do we minister as RCIA team members? Why do we teach others how to live as Christians and as Catholics? Why do we give so much of ourselves to this work?

It is useful to sometimes ask ourselves why we do what we do.

Marketing consultant Simon Sinek, author of *Start With Why: How Great Leaders Inspire Everyone to Take Action*, says that what makes great leaders stand out is their ability to know and say why they do what they do. He lists three levels of how people communicate their purpose in life:

1. Why—This is a person's core belief. It is why you are in the universe.

2. How—This is how you fulfill your goals and dreams.

3. What—This is what you do to accomplish your goals and dreams.

Most people, according to Sinek, focus on what they do. If pushed to go deeper, some people might tell you how they do what they do. Sinek says that a lot of people don't know and can't tell you why they do what they do.

He uses Apple as an example. Imagine that the people at Apple said, We make great computers. That's true. That's what they do.

But what if instead they said, With everything we do, we aim to challenge the status quo. We aim to think differently. That's why we make great computers.

So why do we do what we do? Essentially, our "why" is the same "why" as that of the early disciples. Why did Peter rush out into the streets of Jerusalem to preach about Jesus? He tells us why in the Acts of the Apostles:

- First, he quotes the prophet Joel: "[E]veryone shall be saved who calls on / the name of the Lord" (2:21).

- Then he quotes King David: "You have made known to me the paths of life; / you will fill me with joy in your presence" (2:28).

- And, emboldened by the Spirit, he then speaks for himself: "Repent and be baptized, every one of you, in the name of Jesus Christ for the forgiveness of your sins; and you will receive the gift of the holy Spirit" (2:38).

Why did Paul travel all over the region to tell others about Jesus?

- He tells us why in his First Letter to the Thessalonians: "We were determined to share with you not only the gospel of God, but our very selves as well, so dearly beloved had you become to us" (2:8).

- He explains to the Romans why he is on a mission to share the Good News: "For 'everyone who calls on the name of the Lord will be saved'" (10:13).

- And he reminds the Corinthians of the "why" he had already shared with them: "Now I am reminding you, brothers [and sisters], of the gospel I preached to you, which you indeed received and in which you also stand. Through it you are also being saved, if you hold fast to the word I preached to you (1 Cor 15:1-2).

Matthew, Mark, Luke, John, Peter, Paul, and all the New Testament writers set out to tell the good news that Jesus promises salvation to everyone. Why they did what they did was so no one would be lost; all would be saved. The how and the what were determined by their why.

A New Way

For the first disciples, Jesus was a new thing, a new reality. Jesus was the arrival of a new day, a new way. Jesus turned their world upside down. As we mentioned in the previous section, Luke has Mary sing about this in the *Magnificat*:

> He has thrown down the rulers from their thrones
>   but lifted up the lowly.

A world in which the mighty are thrown down and the lowly are lifted up is not a world that any of the early disciples had ever experienced. It is not a world we had ever experienced. Until Jesus.

Each of the gospel writers tells us that, each through his own lens of experience, as do Peter and Paul:

- Mark introduces us to Jesus in the Jordan River, being baptized by John. As Jesus comes up out of the water, a voice from the heavens says, "You are my beloved Son" (1:1-12).

- In Matthew, we meet Jesus when the magi come to pay him homage (2:1-23).

- Luke first gives us Jesus in a manger—a food trough for sheep (2:1-20).

- John shows us Jesus not as Jesus, but as the Logos who has been with God since the beginning (1:1-18).

- Peter first experiences Jesus as a person who calls Simon—his old self—to a new life (Luke 5:1-11; John 1:35-42).

- Paul encounters the risen Christ as a blinding, flashing light from heaven that knocks him to the ground (Acts 9:1-19).

Each of these "beginnings" of the story of Jesus is a foreshadowing. Each of these beginnings is different, but they all presage the same thing: Jesus is going to turn the tables. The old power regimes are no longer powerful. The new power is in the things of God's reign.

The Inbreaking of God's Reign

The rest of the story, in each gospel, in the life of Peter, in the journeys of Paul, in your life and in mine, is about how the signs of God's reign are breaking into the world. The rest of the story is about how Jesus broke into each of our lives and changed us forever.

In every human life, there is a struggle with power. Those with more power dominate those with less power. Catechetical trainer Joe Paprocki identifies four things that rob us of power:

- sickness

- poverty

- natural disaster

- death

Paprocki says that God alone is powerful enough to overcome the evil inherent in these human realities: "To demonstrate this reality, Jesus devoted his three years of public ministry to performing dramatic action—mighty deeds—that revealed his power over these dark realities. His mighty deeds announce to us an alternate reality in which we are no longer powerless" (*Under the Influence of Jesus*, 29).

What Jesus did for each of the early disciples was break into their lives and eliminate each of their persecutions. He simply took away the power that sickness, poverty, disaster, and death had over them.

Jesus does the same for each of us. Because he is the beloved Son, the adored one, the Logos, the manger-baby, he now has all the power. The evil of the world has no more power.

Why the disciples needed to tell others about Jesus is because most of the world was still suffering under the power of evil. The disciples were bursting with good news—that there is a new reign, a new way, a new life in which we no longer have to suffer from things that have power over us.

Our "why" is the same. Jesus has freed us and healed us from the swindles, shams, and sacrileges that kept us from being who God created us to be. We died to all of that in our baptism. We are now new things—holy things—in the power of Jesus (see Rom 6:3-11).

Why we serve, evangelize, and teach is because much of the world still suffers. We have the amazing good news that the day of suffering is over. If we believe that, we are compelled to do what Jesus did and what the early disciples did to "bring glad tidings to the poor . . . proclaim liberty to captives / and recovery of sight to the blind, / to let the oppressed go free, / and to proclaim a year acceptable to the Lord" (Luke 4:18-19).

Toyota's Five Whys

Focusing on "why" can help us solve difficult problems. Toyota Motor Corporation uses a process called Five Whys. When confronted with a problem or a decision, a team responsible for the solution will gather and ask "why" five times to get at the core of the difficulty.

For example, let's say an RCIA team is concerned because they have few or no inquirers. The team could ask itself "why" five times:

- Why don't we have any inquirers this year?
  No one called or showed up.

- Why did no one call or show up?
  We don't have an effective way of inviting people.

- Why don't we have an effective way of inviting people?
  No one on our team is skilled at reaching out to people outside the parish.

- Why is no one on our team skilled at reaching out to people outside the parish?
  We have never been trained in effective outreach techniques.

- Why haven't we been trained in effective outreach techniques?
  Up until now, it hasn't been a priority.

If the team had stopped at the first why, it would be difficult for them to implement a solution to their problem of having no inquirers. It seems the solution is out of their hands. But once they drill down to the core of the problem, it is clear that they have, so far, not made outreach to potential inquirers a priority. Now they can take steps to solve the root cause and move toward a solution.

Training in Christian Life

Primary proclamation

Do the Five Whys exercise as part of your morning prayer for five days. Ask yourself why you are Catholic, why you want others to know Jesus, why there is still poverty in the world, why Jesus makes a difference in the world today, why your parish can make a difference.

Initiatory catechesis

Ask your seekers why they have hope. Connect their stories to stories in Scripture or stories of the saints. Take the seekers to a celebration of infant baptism. Afterward, reflect on symbols and images of hope that they noticed.

Ongoing catechesis

Choose one of the Scripture stories from "A New Way" above. Read the Scripture together in *lectio divina* style. Using the elements of the story, discuss how Jesus eliminates the power of sickness, poverty, natural disaster, and death. Alternatively, have the group work in pairs and assign each pair a different Scripture story.

Chapter 7

The Climax: Jesus Makes a Difference

The Jesus Sacrifice

Remembering

When people tell the story of Jamila Abdulle, they don't talk about her birth or her childhood. They don't talk about her skills as a cook or how she met and fell in love with her husband. They don't talk about the first seven children she had and how much she loves them.

The story people tell about Jamila is the sacrifice she made for her eighth child, her baby, in the middle of war-torn Mogadishu in 2009. This story is the one they focus on. We'll get to that story in a bit. Before we do, however, let's look at the story of Jesus. When people tell the story of Jesus, what do they focus on?

When the first disciples began to tell the story of Jesus, they didn't start with his birth, as we tend to do. From our twenty-first-century perspective, we think of the gospels chronologically. But the gospels weren't written chronologically. First, there was the story of Jesus's sacrifice—his passion and death. That is the story the early disciples told over and over. It is the story the disciples on the road to Emmaus were telling.

The Death of Jesus Is the Core Story

That story became the bedrock of all the other stories about Jesus. If we were going to make a movie out of the gospels, we would start with the passion, and then do flashbacks to fill in the rest of the story.

The passion and death is the only story that is consistent throughout all four gospels. All four gospel writers are writing to different audiences, and they each have different goals. So the stories they put in their "flashbacks" vary. But the story of the passion is essentially the same in each one.

We said earlier that revelation is always an act of God. And we noted that Pope Francis reminds us that, as the culmination of God's self-revelation, God sent Jesus to us at the exact right time "to reveal his love for us in a definitive way" (Joy of the Gospel, 1).

What we need to understand and make clear for the catechumens is that the "definitive way" Jesus revealed God's love for us was through Jesus's passion and death. That can seem a little morbid to newcomers, and even to lifelong Catholics. Why would Jesus's death be the ultimate revelation of who God is?

To answer that question, we have to enter into the paradox of mystery. Mystery, in the biblical sense, is not a puzzle with a solution. Mystery is a reality that is completely beyond our understanding. Liturgical scholar James Empereur, SJ, says there are three levels of biblical mystery:

> It means first of all, the mystery of God, especially the plan of salvation that God has for the world. This is not accessible to human beings and so must be revealed. . . .
>
> To accomplish this plan, God sent God's son, Jesus Christ. Christ is the key to this mystery. This second level of meaning is the Christ-mystery. In his death and resurrection, the wisdom of God is realized and revealed . . . .
>
> The third level of meaning of mystery is the mystery of Christian liturgy. Mystery here refers to the sacramental and ritual life of the church . . . . In the liturgy the death and resurrection are recalled, not as a mere reminder of things past, but in such a way that the saving mystery of Christ is present to the

worshippers. ("Paschal Mystery," in *The New Dictionary of Theology*, 745–46)

Eucharist Is the Central Place for Remembering

This third level, the ritual revelation of the mystery of God, is one reason the passion story came to be so consistently told. It was told every time the church gathered to celebrate the liturgy. This remembering of the story predated the writing of the New Testament. So by the time Matthew, Mark, Luke, John, and Paul were writing about the Last Supper, their telling of the story was already influenced by the ritual of the liturgy they had been celebrating every week for decades.

From the earliest days, the disciples gathered for a meal "in memory" of Jesus. "Memory" in this sense has a very specific meaning. The Greek word used in the gospels for "memory" or "remembrance" is anamnesis. Anamnesis (which is the opposite of amnesia) is a full remembering. Liturgical scholar Mark R. Francis, CSV, writes,

> In the NT, the use of anamnesis or memorial finds paradigmatic expression in the Pauline and Lucan accounts of the Last Supper when Jesus gives God thanks, breaks bread, and shares wine in the context of a Passover celebration. By identifying his body and blood with these elements and by commanding his disciples to "do this in memory (anamnesis) of me" (see 1 Cor 11:24-25; Luke 22:19), Jesus reinterpreted the Passover celebration that commemorated God's dramatic intervention in human history by freeing Israel from slavery and death in Egypt. ("Remembrance," in *The Collegeville Pastoral Dictionary of Biblical Theology*, 825)

In this passage, Mark Francis uses the word memorial as an alternative to anamnesis, which, in English, might be a better translation than remembering. Memorial is the word we use in the eucharistic prayer to refer to the acclamation we proclaim at the moment we remember Jesus's breaking of the bread and sharing of the cup at the Last Supper. A memorial doesn't just remember something that happened in the past. It remembers or memorializes something significant that still has meaning today. In the Eucharist, Jesus reframed his own story so that it is still happening today.

Jesus Is the New Exodus

The way Jesus reframed his story is very interesting. At the Last Supper, he remembered or memorialized the exodus story of the angel of death passing over the homes of the Israelites and the Israelites passing over the Red Sea into freedom. This is what the Jewish feast of Passover is all about. Jesus was doing what all Jews do, which is to remember the Passover. But Jesus did it with a twist. In his remembering of the story, he identified himself as the New Exodus or the New Passover. He took the symbols of Passover and applied them to himself.

A primary Passover symbol is the lamb. On the night the Israelites were to escape from Egypt, each family sacrificed a lamb and sprinkled the blood of the lamb on their door post as a sign for the angel of death to "pass over" that household. At the Last Supper, Jesus identified himself with the Passover lamb. In the breaking of the bread and the pouring out of the cup, he memorialized both the sacrifice of Passover and the sacrifice he would make on the cross. Scholars think that the last meal that Jesus celebrated with his disciples had elements of the Jewish Passover meal, but was not itself a Passover. That is because in John's gospel, Jesus's death on the cross coincides with the sacrifice of the paschal lamb in the temple (John 19:31). Perhaps sensing that he would not live to celebrate the Passover, he gathered his disciples to share with them a final meal and to instruct them to associate his sacrifice with God's plan of salvation, which they all knew as the Passover and exodus story. Empereur writes,

> Through the cross Christians pass from darkness to the light of God, from the death of this world to the resurrection of a future life, from condemnation from sin to freedom of the children of God. In the cross of Christ the glory of God is now made manifest. ("Paschal Mystery," 746)

The sacrifice of Jesus on the cross is the ultimate revelation of God's love for us because it demonstrates the great self-sacrifice God is willing to make out of love for us. The sacrifice that Jesus made is like the sacrifice Jamila Abdulle made for Sagal, her five-year-old daughter. Sagal was born with a hole in her heart. Sagal was dying. In 2009, there were no doctors in Mogadishu. So Jamila kissed her husband and the seven older children good-bye. Then she picked up Sagal and carried her 1,100 miles for twenty-one days to Kampala, Uganda. From there, she got connected to a hospital run by the United Nations and then a medical center in Phoenix where Sagal received life-saving, open-heart surgery (Nesima Aberra, "Refugee Mothers: Stories of Sacrifice and Love").

Jesus's sacrifice for us is like a mother's sacrifice for her child. Jesus gave his body and blood out of love for us. That is the primary thing we want seekers and catechumens to remember about Jesus. Jesus sacrificed himself out of love for us.

If we forget, we're goners

Fred Craddock and other ministers in Fannin County, Ga., used to take turns serving as the chaplain at the local hospital. One week Fred went by to congratulate the parents of a newborn baby. The whole clan was gathered around the window looking into the nursery at little Elizabeth who at the moment was screaming at the top of her lungs.

Fred noticed the father standing off by himself. Thinking the fellow was anxious about the child's screaming, Fred approached to reassure him that the baby was fine.

"Oh, I know she's not sick," the father replied, "but she's mad as hell." "Why's she mad?" Fred asked. "Well wouldn't you be mad?" asked the father, "One minute you're with God in heaven and the next minute you're in Georgia."

Fred pursued the conversation, "You believe she was with God before she came here?"

"Oh yeah," the father replied.

"You think she'll remember?" Fred asked.

The father thought a moment, "Well, that's up to her mother and me. It's up to the church. We've got to see that she remembers, 'cause if she forgets, she's a goner." (Larry Love, "A Reminder to Remember")

Salvation

We know that Jesus sacrificed himself for us because he loved us. That is his core story. But what was the reason for his sacrifice? What was his "why"? The purpose of Jesus's sacrifice was for our salvation. We use that word salvation a lot. Let's look more deeply at what it means.

Salvation is for everyone. We can sometimes be inappropriately selective about who merits salvation. But we do not control the gift of God's saving act. Pope Francis famously said that even atheists are saved:

The Lord has redeemed all of us, all of us, with the Blood of Christ: all of us, not just Catholics. Everyone! "Father, the atheists?" Even the atheists. Everyone! And this Blood makes us children of God of the first class! We are created children in the likeness of God and the Blood of Christ has redeemed us all! And we all have a duty to do good. And this commandment for everyone to do good, I think, is a beautiful path towards peace. If we, each doing our own part, if we do good to others, if we meet there, doing good, and we go slowly, gently, little by little, we will make that culture of encounter: we need that so much. We must meet one another doing good. "But I don't believe, Father, I am an atheist!" But do good: we will meet one another there. ("Pope at Mass: Culture of Encounter Is the Foundation of Peace")

If, like me, you were raised to believe the only way to get to heaven was to be a good Catholic who avoided sin and regularly confess the sins we did commit, this can be a little confusing. If atheists are saved, what are we doing in the RCIA process? Why bother?

Toward the end of the twentieth century, Pope John Paul II spoke to the United Nations. His goal in that address was to align the spiritual mission of the church with the ideals and goals of the United Nations. Specifically, Pope John Paul wanted to inspire "the whole family of people living on the face of the earth" (1) to make the world more human:

> As a Christian, my hope and trust are centered on Jesus Christ, the two thousandth anniversary of whose birth will be celebrated at the coming of the new millennium. We Christians believe that in his Death and Resurrection were fully revealed God's love and his care for all creation. *Jesus Christ is for us God made man, and made a part of the history of humanity. Precisely for this reason, Christian hope for the world and its future extends to every human person.* . . .
>
> Each and every human person has been created in the "image and likeness" of the One who is the origin of all that is. We have within us the capacities for wisdom and virtue. With these gifts, and with the help of God's grace, we can build in the next century and the next millennium a civilization worthy of the human person, a true culture of freedom. *We can and must do so!* (Address to the United Nations, 17–18)

The reason we bother to bring the first proclamation to the whole world is not just so people will get to heaven. It is to fulfill Jesus's mission to establish God's reign on earth, right here, right now. The role of the church is to work to create "a true culture of freedom."

Every human is made in the image and likeness of God. There is no question that God intends salvation for all. All of us are filled with God's grace, and all of us have the gifts of God's Spirit. Our Christian faith fills us with hope and trust centered on Jesus Christ. And, because we are baptized into Christ, our job—our vocation— is to bring that hope and trust to those who most need it. That is what Pope Francis means by "doing good." We are not called to merely avoid sin. We are compelled to bring the good news of salvation to the world. *"We can and must do so!"* says Pope John Paul II.

Salvation is first of all for the poor. The way we "do good" is by imitating Jesus. Jesus's life was one of love of neighbor and concern for the world. So by looking at how Jesus lived and died, we come to understand what salvation means. Jesus always aligned himself with the underprivileged, the poor, the marginalized, much like the popes are calling us to do. Jesus's death is the supreme example of that. Jesus was willing to enter into suffering and death out of love for us.

As we said earlier, the primary story the first disciples told about Jesus was his passion and death. Their remembering of and reflection on the passion was the beginning of our theology of salvation. The church has distilled four basic truths from their early reflections. In the New Testament, we discover these truths:

1. Salvation is possible only through Jesus Christ. All New Testament writers agree with this.

2. Jesus's sacrifice unilaterally makes amends to God on our behalf.

3. Jesus's obedience to God's will and Jesus's love for us led him to make reparation for our sins.

4. Even though we are saved because of Jesus's sacrifice, we still have a responsibility to seek forgiveness and to repent. (Berard L. Marthaler, *The Creed*, 164.)

These New Testament teachings, as well as the story of God's saving action in the Old Testament, lead us to two basic principles about salvation:

1. God is always faithful to us and always loves us no matter what.

2. God's overwhelming love for us causes God to have a deep compassion for us in our suffering. (Marthaler, 164.)

This can be a conundrum for seekers. They will sometimes ask, If God loves us so much and has so much compassion for us, why does God allow us (or our loved ones or the world) to suffer?

God Does Not Want Us to Suffer

We have to be very clear with seekers that God does not want us to suffer. God wants us to live life fully, without pain or suffering. The reason God sent Jesus to us was to establish a new reign in which "[h]e will wipe every tear from their eyes, and there shall be no more death or mourning, wailing or pain, [for] the old order has passed away" (Rev 21:4).

The church teaches that suffering and death entered the world through sin. Sometimes we bring suffering onto ourselves or others through our own offensive actions. But very often, innocent people suffer for no apparent reason; their suffering cannot be explained. Suffering is part of the human condition. Ultimately, suffering and death are a great mystery. But it is not God's plan or intent that we suffer and die. We must never think that, and we must never allow our seekers to think that.

When Pope Francis visited the Philippines in 2015, twelve-year-old Glyzelle Palomar asked the pope why God allows children to suffer and be victims of horrific crimes. Francis replied, "Only when we too can cry about the things that you said are we able to come close to replying to that question: 'Why do children suffer so much?' Certain realities in life we only see through eyes that are cleansed through our tears." Then he embraced the girl (Eamonn Conway, "The Mystery of Suffering").

How Do We Respond to Suffering?

When we encounter people in pain, we cannot satisfactorily explain the mystery of suffering. We cannot take away their pain. We can assure them that God loves them and God is not punishing them. We can promise them that God did not cause their pain. In fact, God's whole being is about mercy and freedom from suffering. And sometimes, the only way we can say that is to embrace them and cry with them—just as God does with us.

While we cannot completely explain the reason suffering still exists, we can clearly teach what our response to suffering must be. We have to act like Jesus. We have to be the face of mercy toward those who suffer. And we have to do all we can to eradicate suffering from the world.

Sometimes, perhaps most times, alleviating the suffering of others will mean that we will have to suffer ourselves. We will have to sacrifice ourselves at some level in order to bring mercy to others. That is the example Jesus set for us in his suffering and death.

Suffering and hope

To suffer with faith in Christ, abandoning the too-human measure of earthly goods and evils and entrusting oneself into the hands of Christ's father, is to reproduce the pattern of Christ's death. Suffering in that spirit is filled with hope, for it bears the sure promise of resurrection. If we copy Christ's suffering, "he will transfigure these wretched bodies of ours into copies of his glorious body" (Phil 3:21). The Christian in suffering becomes an imitation and an image of Christ—and "if in union with Christ we have imitated his death, we shall also imitate him in his resurrection" (Rom 6:5). (Leonard Bowman, *The Importance of Being Sick*)

Perhaps we cannot completely understand the reason Jesus had to suffer or why any of us have to suffer. But we know from the story of the cross that the evil that causes suffering is not absolute. Jesus's death on the cross is victory over evil. At the very moment when suffering seems to have defeated Jesus—the moment of his death—that is the moment in which he was glorified by the Father. Saint Paul said the world sees Jesus's death on the cross as "foolishness," but "the foolishness of God is wiser than human wisdom, and the weakness of God is stronger than human strength" (1 Cor 1:25).

In the previous section, we explored why the first disciples were so focused on the story of Jesus's passion and death. We said that they never wanted to forget the ultimate sacrifice Jesus made for us and for the world.

In this section, we discovered the reason for Jesus's sacrifice. He sacrificed himself for our salvation and especially for the salvation of the poor and the marginalized. His sacrifice is an example for us of how to live and how to offer our lives for the service of others. In the next section, we will look at the story of Jesus's resurrection.

Examination of conscience

Do I trust God's goodness and providence, even in times of stress and illness?

Do I give in to sickness, to despair, to other unworthy thoughts and feelings?

Do I fill my empty moments with reflection on life and with prayer to God?

Do I accept my illness and pain as an opportunity for suffering with Christ, who redeemed us by his passion?

Do I live by faith, confident that patience in suffering is of great benefit to the Church? (Rite of Penance, Appendix II, 68)

Training in Christian Life

Primary proclamation

Reflect on a time you were brought to life by God's love. Practice telling three versions of your story—thirty seconds, two minutes, and five minutes. Stay alert to times when you can share your story with others.

Initiatory catechesis

Make ample time for each seeker to share their stories of "dying." Connect their stories to stories in Scripture or to the lives of the saints. Celebrate a minor exorcism (RCIA 90–94), and offer a mystagogical reflection afterward.

Ongoing catechesis

Together, read the story of Monsignor Martin Hellriegel in the *United States Catholic Catechism for Adults* (165–66). Discuss together how the liturgy celebrates the paschal mystery.

*   *   *   *   *

The Resurrection

Why is the resurrection important? The answer is not always immediately clear. Remember that even the first disciples were slow to believe that Jesus rose from the dead. If the very people who should have most clearly understood the reason for the resurrection didn't at first believe it, what does that mean for our ability to understand this mystery?

The resurrection of Jesus from the dead is the heart of our belief. Saint Paul said, "[I]f Christ has not been raised, your faith is in vain" (1 Cor 15:17). The reason there is a Christian faith is that we have faith in the resurrection of Christ.

The Centrality of the Resurrection

You might think that's obvious, but the church had not always focused on the mystery of the resurrection as the defining moment of our life in Christ. At times, even in the New Testament era, there had been an emphasis on proving the fact of the resurrection. Some eras of our history had been more concerned about the mystery of the incarnation and what it meant for the Word to become flesh. At other times, the theology of the crucifixion and its meaning for the forgiveness of our sins had taken center stage. And sometimes, even when some theologians did focus on the resurrection, they did so as a way of proving that everything Jesus said was true. The resurrection was, in a sense, the final miracle.

There is nothing wrong with emphasizing any of these teachings, unless they blur our understanding of the resurrection as the foundational teaching that gives meaning to everything else. What we have to understand and what we have to teach seekers is this: the resurrection is not merely proof of the Gospel message; the resurrection is the Gospel message. This key truth was highlighted at the Second Vatican Council:

> As a result, [Jesus] himself—to see whom is to see the Father
> . . . completed and perfected Revelation and confirmed it with
> divine guarantees. He did this by the total fact of his presence
> and self-manifestation—by words and works, signs and mira-
> cles, *but above all by his death and glorious resurrection from the dead,
> and finally by sending the Spirit of truth.* He revealed that God was
> with us, to deliver us from the darkness of sin and death, and
> to raise us up to eternal life. (Constitution on Divine Revelation,
> 4; emphasis added)

The Seven Themes of the Resurrection Stories

Throughout the New Testament, there are several different descriptions of the resurrection. We're not going to go through all of them. But we will spend some time with the final one. It might surprise you that the very last written description of the resurrection is in Mark's gospel. Mark's gospel was the first of the gospels to be written. But the very end of his gospel, 16:9-20, was added on long after Mark and all of the other gospels had been written. And it was added on because if you stop at Mark's original ending, the conclusion is very abrupt:

> Then they went out and fled from the tomb, seized with trembling and bewilderment. They said nothing to anyone, for they were afraid. (16:8)

Without the later addition, Mark's gospel actually says nothing about the resurrection!

In the add-on verses, 9-20, Jesus appears to Mary Magdalene and two other disciples. He later appears to the eleven, and he "rebuked them for their unbelief and hardness of heart because they had not believed those who saw him after he had been raised" (v. 14). He also commissions them to "proclaim the gospel to every creature. Whoever believes and is baptized will be saved" (vv. 15-16). And after he said that, he was taken up into heaven.

In these add-on verses, there are seven themes of the resurrection that summarize all of the resurrection stories:

1. Jesus rose on the first day of the week.

2. Jesus appeared to Mary Magdalene; she was the first disciple to announce the Good News.

3. The disciples were in mourning over Jesus's death.

4. Jesus had so changed in his appearance that he was at first unrecognizable.

5. The disciples were slow to believe Jesus had risen from the dead.

6. Jesus sent the disciples out to proclaim the Good News and to call others to believe in Jesus.

7. Jesus sent his Spirit to make his presence real in the world, even though he was taken up into heaven. (See Marthaler, 181.)

Unrecognizable Jesus

The important point here is the fourth theme—Jesus's changed appearance. Jesus's resurrection was not a resuscitation of his body as was the resurrection of Lazarus. Lazarus came out of the tomb the same way he went into the tomb. No one had difficulty recognizing him. And Lazarus did eventually die.

On the other hand, Jesus's body was radically changed, so much so that he was almost unrecognizable. And his resurrected self was no longer subject to death. In his resurrection, Jesus transcended death. It is also important to note that it was not merely Jesus's "soul" that was resurrected. In the New Testament era, there were two different understandings of human existence. Greek thinkers (many of St. Paul's disciples, for example) believed humans were made up of two separate parts—a body and a soul. The soul was immortal, but the body would eventually die.

Saint Paul, who was Jewish, taught that the body and the soul were different aspects of one whole human being. While they were different, the body and soul could not be separated. So for Christians, belief in the resurrection means the whole human, body and soul, is resurrected.

However, the resurrected person is not the same as the earthly body. Resurrection is not the same as resuscitation of a corpse. Jesus rose to a new life, not his old life. His new life is one that transcends the bounds of time and space.

The man from heaven

Christ's Resurrection was not a return to earthly life, as was the case with the raisings from the dead that he had performed before Easter: Jairus' daughter, the young man of Naim, Lazarus. These actions were miraculous events, but the persons miraculously raised returned by Jesus' power to ordinary earthly life. At some particular moment they would die again. Christ's Resurrection is essentially different. In his risen body he passes from the state of death to another life beyond time and space. At Jesus' Resurrection his body is filled with the power of the Holy Spirit: he shares the divine life in his glorious state, so that St. Paul can say that Christ is "the man of heaven." (*Catechism of the Catholic Church*, 646)

When we are baptized into Christ's death, we will rise with him, not to our old lives, but a new, transcendent life (see Rom 6:3-4). Like Jesus, our risen selves will be radically different in appearance. The church has never defined exactly what that difference is. All we know for sure is that the resurrected Jesus was so transformed as to be almost unrecognizable and that he was no longer bound by physical laws of time and space.

Doubt

Whenever we talk about doubt, Thomas comes to mind. Despite the eyewitness testimony of the other disciples, Thomas was a holdout. Without physical proof, he refused to believe Jesus had risen. Doubters always want more proof. The proof Thomas required was to be able to touch Jesus's physical wounds. But if you read the story closely, when given the opportunity to do so, Thomas never touched the wounds. Simply being in the presence of the risen Christ was enough for Thomas to believe (see John 20:24-29).

Many people today, even people of faith, have doubts. That's part of the human condition. If even those closest to Jesus during his historical life had doubts, how can we hope to believe? How can we lead others to faith in spite of their doubts?

The fact is, we can't. Faith is a gift. Even people of great faith have doubts. Even Mary, when an angel told her she would give birth to Jesus, responded, "How can this be?" (Luke 1:34). Doubt can never be answered with proof or logic. When we believe in someone—our spouse, our child, our mentor, or Jesus—we believe as an act of love. We believe because we have entered into a relationship with the other. Without love and without the gift of the Holy Spirit to open our eyes and ears, we will not be able to recognize Jesus in our midst.

Did Jesus Need to Rise from the Dead?

So why is the resurrection important? Why is it the heart of our belief? Did Jesus even need to rise from the dead?

Jesus did need to rise for the same reason he needed to be born. God chose to become one of us. And in becoming one of us, God revealed to us—intimately and radically—who God is. We know who God is because we know Jesus. Jesus, who is both fully human and fully divine, was born, lived, suffered, died, and rose. In his life, death, and resurrection, we see not only who God is, but who we are meant to be. When we have doubts, we need to recall that God desires to know us and be known by us. The gift of faith is not far away from us; it is deep within our hearts. The resurrection is not meant to test our faith in God, but confirm it. The resurrection is the climactic act of God's self-revelation.

Just as Jesus rose from the dead and transcended the power of death, we too will rise with him. We will share in his resurrection. And on that day, we know we will see God face-to-face, and we will "rejoice with an indescribable and glorious joy" (1 Pet 1:8).

The empty tomb

The empty tomb expresses something vital about the nature of redemption, namely that redemption is much more than a mere escape from our scene of suffering and death. Rather it means the transformation of this material, bodily world with its whole history of sin and suffering. The first Easter began the work of finally bringing our universe home to its ultimate destiny. God did not discard Jesus' earthly corpse, but mysteriously raised and transfigured it so as to reveal what lies ahead for human beings and their world. In short, that empty tomb in Jerusalem is God's radical sign that redemption is not an escape to a better world but an extraordinary transformation of this world. (Gerald O'Collins, SJ, "The Resurrection of Christ," in *The New Dictionary of Theology*, 883)

Training in Christian Life

Primary proclamation

Do you have an experience of recognizing Christ in someone or in some situation that surprised you? Choose a day this week and focus on looking for Christ in unexpected people and places. Challenge yourself to see Christ in the most unlikely person you encounter.

Initiatory catechesis

Ask your seekers if they have ever heard the story of Jesus's resurrection. Ask them to tell you what they have heard. Then read one of the stories from Scripture and compare it to the seekers' stories. (See appendix 2, "Four Amazing Stories of Resurrection.") Celebrate a blessing of the catechumens (RCIA 95–97), and offer a mystagogical reflection afterward.

Ongoing catechesis

Together, in *lectio divina* style, read one of the stories of Jesus's resurrection (see appendix 2, "Four Amazing Stories of Resurrection"). Then read and discuss Pope John Paul II's meditation on the resurrection found in the *United States Catholic Catechism for Adults*, 178–79).

The Jesus Offer

Do you remember when you asked (or got asked), "Will you marry me?" Or how about when your soon-to-be-boss said, "When can you start?" Many of us remember getting accepted to the college of our choice—or not. Some of us remember getting the diagnosis that everything is "normal"—or not. These are the moments that turn our lives upside down. Nothing is ever the same. For better or worse, everything is now brand new.

Earlier, we said that the reason Jesus came was to do a new thing. He intended to turn things upside down. He came to "bring glad tidings to the poor . . . proclaim liberty to captives / and recovery of sight to the blind, / to let the oppressed go free, / and to proclaim a year acceptable to the Lord" (Luke 4:18-19).

And then he died. Jesus's death was a crisis for the disciples. With Jesus gone, who was going to turn the world upside down? Who was going to bring glad tidings, proclaim liberty, free the oppressed, and all that?

The Exciting Climax

What we have been doing in this book is tracing the story of God. That story has three parts, the beginning, the climax, and the end.

We are at the climax point. The death and resurrection of Jesus are very dramatic, important elements of the story. But they are only the lead-up to the climax. The climax is the answer to the disciples' question, What are we going to do now?

In the story of the ascension, Jesus answers that question. For forty days after the resurrection, Jesus had been appearing to the disciples and reminding them about everything he had told them about turning the world upside down. So, naturally, they asked him, "Lord, are you at this time going to restore the kingdom to Israel?" (Acts 1:6). Is today the day you are going to turn everything upside down?

And he more or less said to them, "That's what I trained you to do." Then, as soon as he said that, "he was lifted up, and a cloud took him from their sight" (Acts 1:9). One way to look at the story of the ascension is to say that it marks the beginning of the church's ministry. We tend to think of the ascension as the time when Jesus "left." But that's not exactly correct. A Benedictine monk once told me that Jesus did not so much go "up" as he went "out." I've thought for a long time about what the monk meant by that. I think it means that when Luke says that Jesus "was lifted up, and a cloud took him from their sight" (Acts 1:9), he was saying that Jesus was "lifted" into the entire cosmos. He didn't go away. He went everywhere at once. Jesus was now taken "from their sight," but the church became fully visible as the embodiment of Jesus. The rest of the story told in Acts is what that embodiment looks like. And what it looks like is a Spirit-filled community of disciples that takes to the streets to proclaim the Good News (see Acts 2).

Cloud

Many ancient people believed that the divine presence was such an awe-inspiring splendor that one had to ward it off. Usually the cloud is part of that cosmic scenario that manifests the divine presence but preserves the divine transcendence. The cloud is also a powerful symbol of God's involvement with humans. (John F. Craghan, *The Collegeville Pastoral Dictionary of Biblical Theology*, 148)

Matthew tells the story a little differently. According to him the very last thing Jesus said to the disciples was, "Go, therefore, and make disciples of all nations, baptizing them in the name of the Father, and of the Son, and of the holy Spirit, teaching them to observe all that I have commanded you" (Matt 28:19-20). The bishops of the Second Vatican Council described what this "Great Commission" looks like for our time:

> The mission of the Church is carried out by means of that activity through which, in obedience to Christ's command and moved by the grace and love of the Holy Spirit, the Church makes itself fully present to all men and peoples in order to lead them to the faith, freedom and peace of Christ by the example of its life and teaching, by the sacraments and other means of grace. . . .

Since this mission continues and, in the course of history, unfolds the mission of Christ, who was sent to evangelize the poor, then the Church, urged on by the Spirit of Christ, must walk the road Christ himself walked: a way of poverty and obedience, of service and self-sacrifice even to death, a death from which he emerged victorious by his resurrection. (Decree on the Church's Missionary Activity, 5)

John's account of Jesus's departure is more poetic. The last conversation Jesus had was a private one with Peter. Peter, in this passage, is a symbol of the church. Jesus asks Peter (that is, the church), "Do you love me?" Peter-church says yes. As a symbol of the church, Peter's yes becomes our yes. We, in Peter, declare our love for Christ (in contrast to the earlier triple denial (John 18:17, 25-26). And Jesus gives Peter (us) a task that will turn everything upside down: feed my sheep (see John 21:15-19). The church is now commissioned to look after the flock that the Father had entrusted to Jesus.

Pope Francis elaborated further on this world-changing mission: "Bringing the Gospel is bringing God's power to pluck up and break down evil and violence, to destroy and overthrow the barriers of selfishness, intolerance and hatred, so as to build a new world" (World Youth Day, 2013).

Our mission is disruptive in the same way the mini mills we discussed earlier were. We are called to disrupt the barriers of selfishness, intolerance, and hatred and build something new.

A Once-in-a-Lifetime Offer

All of these stories of Jesus's departure have one thing in common. Jesus is making an offer. He is offering the disciples (and us) a completely new life. The disciples have a choice to make. They can return to their lives as fishermen, tax collectors, and laborers— ordinary people. Or they can change the world. If this were a television movie, the screen would fade, and we'd go to a commercial as we await the exciting conclusion.

Of course, we already know the choice the disciples made. But I don't think they knew it at the time. I don't think it was an easy choice. I think they had to wrestle with it. I think that's true because I have had to wrestle with choices God has asked me to make. So have you. And when you get to the point with your seekers that you make them "the offer," they will have to wrestle with their decision as well.

Do You Love Me?

Jesus asked Peter (and us), "Do you love me?" Pedro Arrupe, SJ, is said to have answered that question this way:

> Nothing is more practical than finding God;
> that is, than falling in love
> in a quite absolute, final way.
> What you are in love with,
> what seizes your imagination, will affect everything.
> It will decide
> what will get you out of bed in the morning,
> what you do with your evenings,
> how you spend your weekends,
> what you read, whom you know,
> what breaks your heart,
> and what amazes you with joy and gratitude.
> Fall in Love, stay in love,
> and it will decide everything.
> (*Finding God in All Things*)

If we say yes to Jesus's offer of love, our lives will never be the same. Everything will be turned upside down. And we're all holding our breath, waiting to know how our seekers will answer.

Because their answer could change the world.

Training in Christian Life

Primary proclamation

Imagine that Pope Francis stops by your house. (It could happen! See http://www.telegraph.co.uk/news/2017/05 /19/pope-francis-surprises-dozen-families-afternoon -visit-homes/). You then ask the pope what you can do to be a better Christian. The pope replies, "Heal the wounds, heal the wounds." How would you put the pope's words into action in your own life?

Initiatory catechesis

Identify four places or activities in your parish where healing happens. Take the seekers to each of them (or divide the seekers into four groups, sending one group to one of the activities). Gather later for a mystagogical reflection on their experience.

Ongoing catechesis

Together read paragraphs 119–21 of Pope Francis's letter Joy of the Gospel. Discuss what it means to be a "missionary disciple."

Chapter 8

The End: Walking the Talk

Everybody Matters

Pope Francis likes to tell the story of the Prodigal Son. Except he doesn't call it that. He calls it the story of the Merciful Father. You know the story. The youngest son rejects his life with his father and goes off into the world where he squanders his inheritance. Broke and hungry, he returns ashamed to his father, hoping to get hired on as a farmworker. The father, while the son is still a long way off, runs to embrace his son and welcome him home. Reflecting on this parable, Pope Francis said,

> The father's mercy is overflowing, unconditional, and shows itself even before the son speaks. Certainly, the son knows he erred and acknowledges it: "I have sinned . . . treat me as one of your hired servants" (Luke 15:18-19). These words crumble before the father's forgiveness. The embrace and the kiss of his father makes him understand that he was always considered a son, in spite of everything. This teaching of Jesus is very important: our condition as children of God is the fruit of the love of the Father's heart; it does not depend on our merits or on our actions, and thus no one can take it away . . .

Jesus' words encourage us never to despair. . . . I think of those who have made mistakes and cannot manage to envision the future, of those who hunger for mercy and forgiveness and believe they don't deserve it. . . . In any situation of life, I must not forget that I will never cease to be a child of God, to be a son of the Father who loves me and awaits my return. Even in the worst situation of life, God waits for me, God wants to embrace me, God expects me. (General Audience, May 11, 2016)

"God expects me." It is precisely when we are broke and broken that God expects us. And it is in that moment of brokenness when Jesus makes us an offer. We can continue to squander our lives, or we can join him in his love relationship with the Father, the God who expects us.

Say Yes to Holiness

As soon as we say yes to Jesus's offer, we enter into a life of holiness. When we say yes to Jesus's love, we are saying yes to becoming the holy person God created us to be (see 1 Thess 4:3 and Eph 1:4).

Saying yes means changing our lives. We give up trying to find joy in worldly things and instead find joy in becoming like Jesus. There is one problem, however. We're not Jesus. Even the best of us fail to live up to our "yes" to Jesus. Pope Francis, for example, said this about himself: "The best summary, the one that comes more from the inside and I feel most true is this: I am a sinner whom the Lord has looked upon" (Spadaro, "A Big Heart Open to God," *America*).

So if even the pope is a sinner, how can any of us be holy? The key is the last part of the pope's description: "whom the Lord has looked upon." Just as the Merciful Father in the Scripture story knew his son had made serious mistakes, the Lord knows that we are all sinners. And it doesn't matter. Pope Francis teaches,

Maybe someone among us here is thinking, My sin is so great, I am as far from God as the younger son in the parable; my unbelief is like that of Thomas. I don't have the courage to go back, to believe that God can welcome me and that he is waiting for me, of all people. But God is indeed waiting for you; he asks of you only the courage to go to him. How many times in my pastoral ministry have I heard it said, "Father, I have many sins"? And I have always pleaded, "Don't be afraid, go to him, he is waiting for you, he will take care of everything." We hear many offers from the world around us; but let us take up God's offer instead: his is a caress of love. For God, we are not numbers, we are important; indeed we are the most important thing to him. Even if we are sinners, we are what is closest to his heart. (Mass for the Possession of the Chair of the Bishop of Rome, April 7, 2013)

What matters to God is not our sin. What matters is that we return. God will run to embrace us as soon as we say yes to his offer. What matters to God is us. You matter. I matter. Everybody matters.

For most of us who are reading this, we have made the big change. We have said yes to Jesus's offer, and we have entered into the love relationship the Father and Son have. The spirit of that relationship—that Holy Spirit—sweeps us up into their love and makes us holy as well. Like the pope, we remain sinners. But as we grow in faith and in love, the sinful part of us becomes less and less and the holy part of us becomes more and more.

Make the Big Change

Some seekers have not yet made the big change. They haven't yet heard Jesus's offer, or they may have heard it and rejected it. Some of them may not think they matter to anyone, much less God.

To accept God's offer means that we participate in God's holiness: "[A]s he who called you is holy, be holy yourselves in every aspect of your conduct, for it is written, 'Be holy because I [am] holy'" (1 Pet 1:15-16). We share in God's holiness because we share in Jesus's holiness. We have been anointed with the same spirit as Jesus, and because of that, we are also holy like Jesus. Like the first disciples, we are sent into the world to do the work that Jesus started—announce God's amazing, life-changing offer.

Our holiness serves a purpose. Its purpose is to make us into people who are so like Christ that people see in us the love that God has to offer them: "Put on then, as God's chosen ones, holy and beloved, heartfelt compassion, kindness, humility, gentleness, and patience, bearing with one another and forgiving one other, if one has a grievance against another; just as the Lord has forgiven [us], so must [we] also do. And over all these put on love, that is, the bond of perfection" (Col 3:12-14).

All of us are called to holiness. The bishops at the Second Vatican Council said,

> [A]ll Christians in any state or walk of life are called to the full-
> ness of Christian life and to the perfection of love . . . In order
> to reach this perfection the faithful should use the strength dealt
> out to them by Christ's gift, so that, following in his footsteps
> and conformed to this image, doing the will of God in every-
> thing, they may wholeheartedly devote themselves to the glory
> of God and to the service of their neighbor. (Dogmatic Constitu-
> tion on the Church, 40)

The Path to Holiness

It is hard to think of ourselves as holy because "holiness" con-jures up images of saints and people who led near-perfect lives. To be holy, we do have to follow and imitate Jesus as best as we can. However, we follow that path by using the gifts God gave us. We become holy in small steps, over a lifetime. It is a process of ongoing conversion in which we become more and more like Christ. And in becoming more like Christ, we become more and more who God made us to be.

If we focus on our inadequacies and personal failings, it will be difficult for us to live as God intended us to. The path to holiness means leaving behind our self-preoccupation and self-absorption by dying to our old selves (Gal 2:20). Using our gift of holiness, we set out to find those who most desperately need God's love. To be holy means loving the least among us—the people on the peripheries who have been marginalized by all the things the world considers valuable.

Because, like the son in the Scripture story, even in the depths of their brokenness, the least among us matter to God. And because they matter to God, they also matter to us. Everybody matters.

Living this life of holiness is what we mean by discipleship. All of us become disciples at our baptism, but there is a secret to actually living as a disciple. That's what we will look at in the next section.

Training in Christian Life

Primary proclamation

Always treat strangers with respect. Ask waitstaff and cashiers their names and give them yours. Make eye contact with homeless people on the street when you encounter them. Pray for the Holy Spirit to lead you into a meaningful conversation with a stranger.

Initiatory catechesis

Tell stories of saints who were rejected by the world. Engage the seekers in ministry to shut-ins and food pantries. Gather together afterward for a mystagogical reflection.

Ongoing catechesis

Read together from Pope Francis's exhortation Joy of the Gospel, especially paragraphs 20–24. Discuss the implications of his message for living out your faith.

* * * * *

The Secret to Discipleship

I have a friend who pays twenty dollars a month to belong to a gym. And he doesn't go to the gym. Ever. My friend's gym has about 6,500 members. If just a fourth of the members showed up to exercise, there would be no room. Imagine if they all showed up. My friend's gym knew when they signed him up that they probably wouldn't be seeing much of him. That's because he, like most of us, lacks the discipline to exercise.

Sometimes I think our parishes are selling gym memberships. We know the seekers who sign up for RCIA (or confirmation or First Communion or marriage prep) won't be around long. We know that after we baptize them, we probably won't see them again. My friend likes the idea of belonging to a gym without actually doing disciplined exercise. Likewise, lots of people like the idea of belonging to a church without actually doing discipleship.

This isn't just true of seekers. It is also true for many lifelong Catholics. It is true for some Catholics who come to church every Sunday, sit in the front pew, serve on the parish council, and coordinate the parish banquet.

If you belonged to a gym, you could go into the gym every week and never exercise. You could attend or teach a course on the benefits of exercise. You could serve on the gym's advisory board about how to maintain and run the gym. You could get hired as a receptionist, accountant, salesperson, or even president of the gym. You could do all of that and never actually lift a weight or run on a treadmill.

We have a lot of Catholics like that. We may go to church, but many of us don't do the essential work of the church. The secret to discipleship is not just being a member of the church. Discipleship is doing what Jesus asked us to do—make more disciples (see Matt 28:19-20).

There is an important difference between making Catholics and making disciples. It is akin to the difference between making gym members and making gym members who exercise. Our goal is to make Catholics who evangelize. According to Pope Francis, there are three keys to Catholic discipleship:

1. "The primacy of witness"

2. "The urgency of going out to meet others"

3. "The need for a pastoral plan centered on the essential" (See Address to Participants in the Plenary of the Pontifical Council for Promoting New Evangelization, October 14, 2013.)

1. Primacy of Witness

The "primacy of witness" requires two things: live like Jesus and talk about Jesus. To live like Jesus means making God's mercy real for everyone who suffers. Just as Jesus did, we have to make the tenderness and compassion of God real for people today. This requires true courage. To be a person of tenderness in today's world is countercultural. To say and do things that offer mercy to the least among us is not considered "normal" by most people. But that is what Jesus did, and it is what we must do. Pope Francis says,

> Every baptized Christian is a "Christopher," namely a Christ-bearer, as the Church Fathers used to say. Whoever has encountered Christ like the Samaritan woman at the well cannot keep this experience to himself but feels the need to share it and to lead others to Jesus (cf. Jn 4). We all need to ask ourselves if those who encounter us perceive the warmth of faith in our lives, if they see in our faces the joy of having encountered Christ! (Address to Pontifical Council for Promoting New Evangelization, October 14, 2013)

We have to live like Jesus, and we also have to talk about Jesus. To talk about Jesus is to say out loud why we live the way we do. If we truly live like Jesus, we will be living in contradiction to many of the things the world finds valuable. And we will be joyful about it! This will raise questions. When people ask us questions, we have to be able to answer with a proclamation of our faith in Jesus.

2. Urgency of Going Out to Meet Others

Pope Francis has said this over and over again. We cannot remain walled up within our churches. The people with the greatest need for God's mercy are not in our churches. They are out on the peripheries of society. Jesus said go and make disciples. He did not say wait here until disciples show up. The pope teaches,

> Here we pass to the second aspect: encounter, *going out to meet others*. . . . This dynamism is part of Christ's great mission to bring life to the world, to bring the Father's love to mankind. The Son of God "went forth" from his divine condition and came to meet us. The Church abides within this movement; every Christian is called to go out to meet others, to dialogue with those who do not think as we do, with those who have another faith or who have no faith. . . .
>
> No one is excluded from life's hope, from God's love. The Church is sent to reawaken this hope everywhere, especially where it has been suffocated by difficult and oftentimes inhuman living conditions; where hope cannot breathe it suffocates. (Address to Pontifical Council for Promoting New Evangelization, October 14, 2013)

3. Pastoral Plan Centered on the Essential

If you look at the ads for my friend's gym, you won't see any weights or challenging equipment in the pictures. You will see very attractive, fit people standing around talking to each other. But you won't see any actual exercise going on. In fact, if you walk into my friend's gym, the weights and the climbing machines are in the back. What you see right up front is a food and juice bar with couches! And a big-screen TV. And fancy workout clothes you can buy. It's like a mini-mall.

Our parishes do something similar. We have lots of activities that distract us from the primary mission. We have to resist the diversions and stay focused on the primary mission. Pope Francis says,

> [T]his cannot be left to chance or improvisation. It requires a shared commitment to a pastoral plan which brings us back to

the essential and which is *solidly focused on the essential; that is, on Jesus Christ.* To get diverted by many secondary or superfluous things does not help; what helps is to focus on the fundamental reality, which is the encounter with Christ, with his mercy and with his love, and to love our brothers and sisters as he has loved us. . . . We might ask ourselves: what is the pastoral plan of our dioceses or parishes like? Does it make the essential visible, namely Jesus Christ? (Address to Pontifical Council for Promoting New Evangelization, October 14, 2013)

This book is all about teaching the essentials in a way that makes not just Catholics, but Catholic disciples. Pope Francis is asking us to focus on the essentials in this time of profound crisis. To do otherwise is just building Catholic juice bars with comfortable couches. The pope reminds us,

Jesus said: Go out and tell the good news to everyone. Go out and in my name embrace life as it is, and not as you think it should be. Go out to the highways and byways, go out to tell the good news fearlessly, without prejudice, without superiority, without condescension, to all those who have lost the joy of living. Go out to proclaim the merciful embrace of the Father. Go out to those who are burdened by pain and failure, who feel that their lives are empty, and proclaim the folly of a loving Father who wants to anoint them with the oil of hope, the oil of salvation. Go out to proclaim the good news that error, deceitful illusions and falsehoods do not have the last word in a person's life. Go out with the ointment which soothes wounds and heals hearts.

Mission is never the fruit of a perfectly planned program or a well-organized manual. Mission is always the fruit of a life which knows what it is to be found and healed, encountered and forgiven. Mission is born of a constant experience of God's merciful anointing. (Holy Mass and Canonization of Blessed Fr. Junípero Serra, September 23, 2015)

We have one more "essential" to talk about, which is how we make Jesus Christ visible to the world. That is the subject of the next section.

Training in Christian Life

Primary proclamation

Find a "highway and byway" in your life where you can tell the Good News fearlessly. For example, contact a family member you have a dispute with. Or volunteer some time with a community you might be wary of, such as people of another religion, youth who live in gang neighborhoods, or people in drug rehabilitation centers. Pray for each of the people you encounter.

Initiatory catechesis

Share gospel stories of times Jesus crossed boundaries in ways that upset institutional leaders. Celebrate a rite of Anointing of the Catechumens (RCIA 98–103), and engage in mystagogical reflection following the rite.

Ongoing catechesis

Discuss the seven themes of Catholic social teaching (do an online search of "USCCB social teaching").

* * * * *

Announce the Good News

At the beginning of this book, we said there are three steps for teaching the core of the faith:

1. Have faith and remain joyful in that faith.

2. Make telling the story of Jesus our number-one priority.

3. Tell the story first of all and always to the poor.

And we said the story has three big parts:

1. The beginning

2. The climax

3. The end

We began this book by reminding ourselves that Pope Francis said there is no place in the church for sourpusses. We cannot let the "bad news" that surrounds us every day defeat the good news of healing and liberation Jesus has to offer. We must have faith in God's promises, and we must always radiate the joy our faith brings us.

God Is Madly in Love with Us

Next we looked at the promises God has made to us. God's first promise (and only promise, really) is that God is madly in love with us and will always be madly in love with us, no matter what.

God is so in love with us, God even gets jealous! "Or do you suppose that the scripture speaks without meaning when it says, 'The spirit that he has made to dwell in us tends toward jealousy'?" (Jas 4:5). The *Catechism of the Catholic Church* says, "That our God is 'jealous' for us is the sign of how true his love is" (2737).

Any promise God has ever made flows from that first promise to love us always. The ultimate proof that God loves us is that God became one of us.

Jesus—Our Best Story

The story of God becoming one of us is our best story. It is the Jesus story. Jesus turned the world (and our lives) upside down. In every human life, there is a struggle with power. Jesus made the powerful weak and the weak powerful. Jesus simply eliminates the power of evil in our lives. And in turn, he turns our weakness into power (see 2 Cor 12:9).

The way that Jesus did this is he sacrificed. He gave his life to all of us, but most of all to "the poor and the sick, those who are usually despised and overlooked" (Pope Francis, Joy of the Gospel, 48). The ultimate sacrifice Jesus made was to die for us. But not even death could defeat him. By the power of God's Holy Spirit, Jesus was raised from the dead. Through his resurrection, he imparted his Spirit to us to continue his mission of bringing healing and liberation to the whole world. It is a continuation of God's promise to always be madly in love with us.

Change the World

So here we are, filled with the joy of our faith, confident in the story of how Jesus sacrificed so much for us. What's next?

We have to go out and turn the world upside down. Pope Francis said,

> If something should rightly disturb us and trouble our consciences, it is the fact that so many of our brothers and sisters are living without the strength, light and consolation born of friendship with Jesus Christ, without a community of faith to support them, without meaning and a goal in life. (Joy of the Gospel, 49)

People are living without light. Without the friendship of Jesus. Job one is to bring light. And we cannot do that from within the walls of our parishes. The pope quoted the Latin American bishops:

> Along these lines the Latin American bishops stated that we "cannot passively and calmly wait in our church buildings"; we need to move "from a pastoral ministry of mere conservation to a decidedly missionary pastoral ministry." (Joy of the Gospel, 15)

It is this "going out" part that seems especially difficult for many of us. It is comfortable to stay within the walls of the parish, among like-minded people, doing ministry, catechesis, and liturgy. These are all good things. But if none of it results in bringing hope to those with no hope, what is the point?

How do we do that? How do we get "outside" our church buildings and become true missionaries?

Five Ways to Go Outside

In Joy of the Gospel, Pope Francis identifies five ways that will get us "outside." Some of these we have already mentioned. I am listing them here—from easiest to hardest—as a training template for our RCIA processes. I believe that all parishioners need to be involved in these evangelizing activities, and RCIA team members need to lead the way.

Some of us might be thinking we signed up to teach, not to evangelize. But actively proclaiming Jesus Christ, especially to those who most need to hear good news, is our most effective form of teaching. Seekers will learn to be missionary disciples by observing our behavior.

1. Don't be a sourpuss. As we have said, we must remain joyful. "One of the more serious temptations which stifles boldness and zeal is a defeatism which turns us into querulous and disillusioned pessimists, 'sourpusses'" (85). The pope also says that we "must never look like someone who has just come back from a funeral! Let us recover and deepen our enthusiasm, that 'delightful and comforting joy of evangelizing'" (10). Feeling and looking joyful is the first step toward getting outside ourselves and focused on others.

2. Talk to people who don't know Jesus. If we are honest, almost all the people in our RCIA processes already know Jesus. We do a great job helping people deepen their relationship to Jesus. That is a very good thing. But it should not be the first thing. Pope Francis says, "We cannot forget that evangelization is first and foremost about preaching the Gospel to *those who do not know Jesus Christ or who have always rejected him*" (14). Perhaps we can challenge ourselves to revise what we do as RCIA teams so we are more diligently reaching out to those who need to hear the Gospel for the very first time.

3. Be patient. Initiation ministry is messy. If you are like me, you don't like messy. I hate messy. I want people to show up on time, give some sign of making progress, and would it hurt to show a little gratitude? Pope Francis nails me on this. He says that yes, Christian ministry is joyful. But it is also cross-full. Sometimes we have to bear the cross of people's messy lives and recognize that the Holy Spirit is working in the midst of the mess. We cannot give in to "the temptation to separate, before its time, the wheat from the weeds; it is the fruit of an anxious and self-centered lack of trust" (85). He also says, "Evangelization consists mostly of patience and disregard for constraints of time" (24).

4. We don't have to teach everything all at once. This should be obvious, but if the pope thought it was important enough to put in his first apostolic exhortation, you have to wonder. Think of it this way. If you have children, you want to teach them not to run out into traffic. You also want to teach them not to fight with their siblings. And you want to teach them not to leave their shoes in the living room. Now, of all those "truths," what is first and most important on your teaching list?

Pope Francis reminds us that there is a "hierarchy of truths." He also reminds us of what is first on the teaching list, which is what we have been emphasizing in this book: "What counts above all else is 'faith working through love.'" And right there next to faith and love is mercy. He quotes Aquinas: "Thomas thus explains that, as far as external works are concerned, mercy is the greatest of all the virtues: 'In itself mercy is the greatest of the virtues, since all the others revolve around it and, more than this, it makes up for their deficiencies'" (37).

5. Go out to the poor. This is a tough one. Pope Francis isn't just talking about volunteering at the soup kitchen or donating a turkey at Thanksgiving. He says we have created an entire economy that treats human beings like "consumer goods to be used and then discarded." He goes on to say,

> We have created a "throw away" culture which is now spreading. It is no longer simply about exploitation and oppression,

but something new. Exclusion ultimately has to do with what it means to be a part of the society in which we live; those excluded are no longer society's underside or its fringes or its disenfranchised—they are no longer even a part of it. The excluded are not the "exploited" but the outcast, the "leftovers." (53)

I don't know how to solve this. I don't know what RCIA teams need to do about it. But it seems central to what we do. If we are the ones who bring "good news" to the world, it seems to me that we have to find a way to make the news "good" for those who are outcast. I'll be praying about this, and examining my own life.

Training in Christian Life

Primary proclamation

Choose one of the "Five Ways to Go Outside" from above, and resolve to practice it daily for a month. Do a nightly examination of conscience to review how you did that day.

Initiatory catechesis

Tell stories from the Acts of the Apostles about ways in which the early disciples remained joyful. Take the seekers to both a wedding and a funeral in your parish. Reflect on the contrasting experiences of joy in both celebrations.

Ongoing catechesis

Choose one of the eucharistic prayers and read it together in *lectio divina* style. Reflect together on the elements of the eucharistic prayer that echo the "Five Ways to Go Outside" above.

Conclusion

We began with Pope Francis's warning that the moral teaching of the church is at risk of collapsing like a house of cards. When we fail to preach the Gospel, and instead focus on "certain doctrinal or moral points," we are weakening the edifice of the church.

This seems like a contradiction. If the moral teaching of the church is at risk, shouldn't we double down on teaching "doctrinal or moral points"? This is exactly the conclusion some parish leaders and RCIA teams have come to. It is usually expressed in terms such as "How do we make sure they know enough?" or "Where can we find a comprehensive curriculum?" or "When do we teach them about _____?"

When our concerns of faith are so small, we devolve into teaching facts instead of revealing the person of Christ. We become rule-bearers instead of Christ-bearers. Pope John Paul II said that as teachers of the faith, our definitive aim "is to put people not only in touch but in communion, in intimacy, with Jesus Christ: only he can lead us to the love of the Father in the Spirit and make us share in the life of the Holy Trinity" (On Catechesis in Our Time, 5).

Pope Francis makes the same point in the "house of cards" passage we quoted earlier:

> Before all else, the Gospel invites us to respond to the God of love who saves us, to see God in others and to go forth from ourselves to seek the good of others. Under no circumstance can

this invitation be obscured! All of the virtues are at the service of this response of love. If this invitation does not radiate forcefully and attractively, the edifice of the Church's moral teaching risks becoming a house of cards, and this is our greatest risk. It would mean that it is not the Gospel which is being preached, but certain doctrinal or moral points based on specific ideological options. The message will run the risk of losing its freshness and will cease to have "the fragrance of the Gospel." (Joy of the Gospel, 39)

Linking the messages of the two popes, we can say that the method for bringing people into intimacy with Jesus Christ is by keeping our message fresh and smelling like the Gospel. The phrase "fragrance of the Gospel" is not footnoted in Joy of the Gospel. It likely comes from St. Paul:

> But thanks be to God, who always leads us in triumph in Christ and manifests through us the odor of the knowledge of him in every place. For we are the aroma of Christ for God among those who are being saved and among those who are perishing, to the latter an odor of death that leads to death, to the former an odor of life that leads to life. Who is qualified for this? For we are not like the many who trade on the word of God; but as out of sincerity, indeed as from God and in the presence of God, we speak in Christ. (2 Cor 2:14-17)

Knowing Christ, in the intimate sense Pope John Paul II speaks of, imbues us with a life-giving fragrance (although it does not seem so to those who reject Christ's offer of life). Saint Paul, knowing the answer, asks, Who is sufficient to go out into the world smelling like Christ? None of us, if we are simply like those "who trade on the word of God." If we simply want to deliver the facts without risking intimacy, we will be insufficient for the task.

However, if we stand in Christ's presence when we teach—if we are sincere enough and vulnerable enough to let our intimacy with Christ shine through—we will be speaking as Christ speaks. We will smell like Christ.

The crisis of misery in the world today and the potential threat of the moral teaching of the church collapsing like a house of cards is why Pope Francis's image of the church as a field hospital is so apt. I think in many places his image is more aspirational than actual. To extend the metaphor, it is as though we are surrounded by people who are bleeding out. Instead of applying tourniquets, we lecture them about the values of a proper diet and regular exercise.

As we said when we started, "The centrality of the kerygma calls for stressing those elements which are most needed today" (Joy of the Gospel, 165). For our message to be fresh and fragrant,

> it should not impose the truth but appeal to freedom; it should be marked by joy, encouragement, liveliness and a harmonious balance which will not reduce preaching to a few doctrines which are at times more philosophical than evangelical. (Joy of the Gospel, 165)

The core of this book is an exploration of those elements of the moral teaching of the church that the world most needs to hear today, which Pope Francis calls the first proclamation or the kerygma:

1. The beginning: Know who God is
   A. The most important lesson seekers must learn
   B. God became one of us
   C. What Jesus did and why it matters

2. The climax: Jesus makes a difference
   A. The Jesus sacrifice
   B. The resurrection
   C. The Jesus offer

3. The end: Walking the talk
   A. Everybody matters
   B. The secret to discipleship
   C. Announce the Good News

That is our curriculum. It is the answer to the concerns of "How do we make sure they know enough?" or "Where can we find a comprehensive curriculum?" or "When do we teach them about _____?"

There is a real risk in this kind of teaching. If we do not control the learning environment and we do not focus on those few doctrines that Pope Francis says "are at times more philosophical than evangelical," we run the risk of change. Our seekers might change, our RCIA process might change, our parish might change. We might change. For most of us, change is scary. It involves dying and rising—and we're not always certain about the "rising."

But the alternative to change—to conversion—is certain death, with no possibility of resurrection. That is a much greater risk.

So, imagine what might happen if we did this. What if? What if we became field hospital catechists? What if we took our charism of healing out onto the battlefield and started proclaiming love and salvation? What if we risked descending into the pain and ugliness in the world and brought beauty into it? Pope Francis holds out a vision for us if we can gather the courage to do it:

> Proclaiming Christ means showing that to believe in and to follow him is not only something right and true, but also something beautiful, capable of filling life with new splendor and profound joy, even in the midst of difficulties. Every expression of true beauty can thus be acknowledged as a path leading to an encounter with the Lord Jesus. (Joy of the Gospel, 167)

Saint Paul asks, "Who is qualified for this?" You are—as long as you do what we ask the seekers to do: Put your trust in Christ.

Appendix 1

A Simple, Low-Risk Plan for "Going Out"

Avanti! That's what Pope Francis says over and over again. Go forth! For Francis, there is only one image of the church that is life-giving—a church that goes forth, that goes out of itself, into the streets. The pope wants us to be a church that goes to the peripheries.

This is a crucial point for RCIA teams. Too often, we stay inside the church and wait for someone to knock on the door. But Pope Francis says that when we do that, we might actually be keeping Jesus inside the church:

> In Revelation, Jesus says that he is at the door and knocks. Obviously, the text refers to his knocking from the outside in order to enter, but I think about the times in which Jesus knocks from within so that we will let him come out. (Pre-conclave address to the General Congregation meetings of the cardinals)

How do we do that? How do we let Jesus out? Where are the peripheries? How do we get there? The simple answer is, wherever you are not going now is probably a periphery. Wherever you are afraid to go or too busy to go or uninterested in going is probably a periphery. Wherever the pain is the greatest and your skills are the most useless is probably a periphery. Wherever the boundary is in your life, the other side is probably a periphery.

But I promised you low-risk. To take a simple first step, try inviting people from the peripheries in before you start going out. Once you have built up a little confidence, you can try physically going out to places that are peripheries for you.

I've created five examples of invitations we might make to people who might be seeking a deeper spirituality in their lives. Some of these audiences might be "inside" the church, and most are "outside." I wrote invitations for:

- Spiritual-but-not-religious people

- Newly divorced people

- Seriously ill people

- Grieving people

- Newly engaged couples

I also tied most of these messages into the holiday season, because that is often a time when those without hope are most attuned to their loneliness. However, these invitations can be easily adapted to other times of the year.

Spiritual-but-Not-Religious

Discover how to be a "Good Samaritan" this holiday season without being a religious bore. Drop in on our no-strings-attached discussion group, and learn about a few universal spiritual practices that have guided Jesus, Buddha, Gandhi, Mother Teresa, and Pope Francis. Find out how you can put these practices to use in your life to have truly happy holidays. We meet every Tuesday at 7 p.m. in the back room of the Melting Pot Grill. Text 000-000-0000 if you need directions or a ride.

Newly Divorced

The holidays are tough for divorced people. But this can also be a time to find hope and even joy. Come gather with several other seekers who want to live a spiritual life but aren't finding the support they need in traditional religious settings. A separation from a marriage partner doesn't have to mean separation from God. Choose a path that will lead you to a deep peace and profound joy. We meet every Wednesday at 7 p.m. in the Pacific Room of the Riverside Community Center. Click here for a Google map or email jim.thompson@email.com for directions.

Seriously Ill

We want to pray with you for healing and strength this holiday season. At our weekly gathering, we share ideas for remaining hopeful, finding peace, resolving fear, and managing stress. Come share your life experience and wisdom, and hear from others who share what you are going through. (Or send us a request for prayers if you cannot be there.) Every evening includes a time of prayer and quiet meditation. We usually start around 7 p.m. on Thursdays in the Sullivan Center Chapel. Just drop in or call or email Jenny Alvarez for more information. 000-000-0000 jalvarez@email.org

Grieving

Come struggle with others to get through the holidays without your loved one. This gathering is a safe place to cry, grieve, talk, doubt, and lament. Some of us believe God comforts us in our grief, and others of us are angry that God failed us. Come as you are, share if you wish, or just sit with others who are also in pain. We will meet at 7 p.m. every Monday of November and December. Come to the O'Malley Center main door (51st and Maple), and follow the signs. Or call or email Virginia Nguyen for more information. 000-000-0000 nguyen7832@email.net

Newly Engaged

Congratulations on your engagement! My name is Deacon Ron Jones, and I'd like to invite you to a series of three open-ended discussions with other newly engaged couples. Usually we discuss things like:

Do I have to be Catholic to get married here?

What if my partner is more religious than I am?

Do we fight too much?

What if I don't fit in with my partner's family?

How do we stay passionate for each other for life?

But that's just a sample. Really, we talk about whatever is on your mind as you prepare for your marriage. We are going to schedule times and dates for these three meetings based on your availability. Click here to let me know when you are free, and I'll get back to you with details: http:// website.com/

Appendix 2

Four Amazing Stories of Resurrection

Mark 16:1-8

Incredibly, we have no eyewitness account of the resurrection anywhere in Scripture. What the disciples attest to is the empty tomb and the post-resurrection appearances of Jesus. Mark's account of the resurrection is perhaps the starkest. In its original form, it ends so abruptly that later editors felt the need to fill in the story.

The original ending is verse 8: "Then [the women] went out and fled from the tomb, seized with trembling and bewilderment. They said nothing to anyone, for they were afraid." Verses 9-20, which were added later, recount the appearances of Jesus to Mary Magdalene and the other disciples and Jesus's ascension.

Why would the original author end his gospel with the witnesses to the empty tomb being too afraid to tell anyone? One possible explanation is the writer was emphasizing what it means to be human. "The resurrection does not mean that Jesus becomes God. Rather it means that the deepest potential of his human nature has been brought to fulfillment in that relation with God that began already at the start of his human life" (Zachary Hayes, "Resurrection: Pastoral-Liturgical Tradition," in *The Collegeville Pastoral Dictionary of Biblical Theology*, 840).

This is indeed good news for us and especially for the seekers we encounter. It is by being fully human that we will enter into a saving relationship with God. If Jesus is resurrected by the power of God (and not under his own power), it means that we too can be redeemed by that same power.

Matthew 28:1-20

Matthew's account of the resurrection is much more dramatic and colorful than Mark's. He has an earthquake, lightning, snow, and a flying angel all besieging the two Marys as they approach the tomb. In an act of inhuman strength, the angel rolls away the boulder that sealed the tomb. The guards (only Matthew has guards) faint from terror. And after all that, the angel says to the women, "Do not be afraid."

Matthew is describing in graphic terms how crucial the resurrection is in God's story. "God is then seen to be truly the Lord of the living and the dead whose life-giving power transcends the power of death. . . . This lies at the heart of the Christian hope for a positive outcome for life" (Hayes, "Resurrection," 840).

The message for our seekers is that their lives are about to undergo seismic shifts. There may be boulders and guards that will block their way. There may be ground-shaking changes as they begin to live as redeemed people. But no matter how hard or how drama-filled the journey may be, they need not fear.

Luke 24:1-53

Mark and Matthew both describe Jesus's appearances to the disciples as taking place in Galilee. For Luke, however, Jerusalem is the place of Jesus's destiny and the place from which the church will fulfill Jesus's mission. So in Luke's gospel, Jesus's appearances take place only in Jerusalem (and on the road to Emmaus, near Jerusalem).

Luke also gives a larger role to the women followers of Jesus. As in Mark and Matthew, it is the women who discover the empty tomb. If you read only Matthew, however, it would seem that only the two Marys were at the tomb. By contrast, Luke identifies "Mary Magdalene, Joanna, and Mary the mother of James; [and] the others who accompanied them" (v. 10). And so, when this small crowd of women all tell the men what they witnessed at the tomb, Luke's comment that the women's testimony "seemed like nonsense [to the men] and they did not believe them" is a strong caution to his own community (and ours).

Luke's gospel is filled with metaphor. While his emphasis on the importance of women to the Christian mission is no doubt rooted in the struggles of actual women in the early church, his description of their dismissal is also symbolic of all who are on the peripheries. "If the language of resurrection is finally a metaphor of salvation, it is a Christian statement about the nature of the reign of God preached by Jesus. The metaphor opens a vision of the ultimate possibilities of human existence. It suggests a vision of a transformed world . . . The call of love lies at the heart of all dreams of a world characterized by peace, justice, and the fullness of life" (Hayes, "Resurrection," 840–41).

For our seekers, Luke's story of the resurrection offers both hope and challenge. The hope is that whatever the world might think of us or however small we might think ourselves to be, we are front-of-the-line beneficiaries of God's saving grace. The challenge is that our status is never an elevation over others but always a call to serve others.

John 20:1-29

John's gospel is filled with images of darkness and light. His story of the resurrection begins in the dark because the disciples have not yet fully experienced the light of faith. While John must have known of the other women who approached the tomb that day, his sole emphasis on Mary Magdalene both certifies her importance to the early church and also serves as a symbol of the entire church. Mary, still in darkness, had "seen" Jesus. But he had been so transformed by the resurrection that he was only recognizable through the eyes of faith. As soon as Jesus said Mary's name, her eyes were opened, and she recognized him.

John's gospel is sometimes described as the most mystical of all the gospels. Having been written much later than the other three, it tends to emphasize the transcendent nature of Jesus. But Jesus's transcendence is not something we are waiting to access in a future life. "The mystery of Christ's resurrection is understood not as a movement to another world but as the beginning of a new relation of Christ to this world" (Hayes, "Resurrection," 841). Mary Magdalene did not need to first undergo her own resurrection to see Jesus. She needed to be reminded of the love she had for him.

This is a powerful message for our seekers. When we hand on to them the promise of eternal life, we are not offering them some pie-in-the-sky future reality. We are offering them life right now. As soon as Jesus calls their names, they are in a new relationship with the reality around them. They are made new.

Bibliography

Aberra, Nesima. "Refugee Mothers: Stories of Sacrifice and Love." International Rescue Committee (IRC). https://web.archive.org/web/2015 0906192619/http://www.rescue.org/us-program/us-phoenix-az /refugee-mothers-stories-sacrifice-and-love.

"Amish Bury 5th Victim as More Details Emerge." *Associated Press*. October 6, 2006. http://www.nbcnews.com/id/15154150/ns/us_news-life/t /amish-bury-th-victim-more-details-emerge/#.WeTik2hSyUk.

Arrupe, Pedro. *Finding God in All Things: A Marquette Prayer Book*. Milwaukee: Marquette University Press, 2005.

Benedict XVI, Pope. *Deus Caritas Est*. December 25, 2005. http://w2.vatican.va /content/benedict-xvi/en/encyclicals/documents/hf_ben-xvi_enc _20051225_deus-caritas-est.html.

———. *Sacramentum Caritatis*. Post-Synodal Apostolic Exhortation on the Eucharist as the Source and Summit of the Church's Life and Mission. February 22, 2007. http://w2.vatican.va/content/benedict-xvi/en /apost_exhortations/documents/hf_ben-xvi_exh_20070222_sacra mentum-caritatis.html.

Boselli, Goffredo. *The Spiritual Meaning of the Liturgy: School of Prayer, Source of Life*. Translated by Barry Hudock. Collegeville, MN: Liturgical Press, 2014.

Bowman, Leonard J. *The Importance of Being Sick: A Christian Reflection*. Wilmington, NC: Consortium, 1976.

Catechism of the Catholic Church. 2nd ed. United States Catholic Conference— Libreria Editrice Vaticana, 1997.

Congregation for the Clergy. *General Directory for Catechesis*. Washington, DC: United States Catholic Conference, 1998.

Conway, Eamonn. "The Mystery of Suffering." *The Irish Catholic*. http://www.irishcatholic.ie/article/mystery-suffering.

Craghan, John F. "Cloud." In *The Collegeville Pastoral Dictionary of Biblical Theology*, edited by Carroll Stuhlmueller and Dianne Bergant, 148–50. Collegeville, MN: Liturgical Press, 1996.

Curry, Ann. "Amish Display the True Meaning of Forgiveness." *NBC News*. October 4, 2006. http://www.nbcnews.com/id/15134030/ns/nbc_nightly_news_with_brian_williams/t/amish-display-true-meaning-forgiveness/#.WeTfbmhSyUk.

DeBlieu, Jan. "Using Your Grief to Help Others—and Heal Yourself." *The Huffington Post*. December 21, 2015. http://www.huffingtonpost.com/jan-deblieu/using-your-grief-to-help-others--and-heal-yourself_b_8545308.html.

Empereur, James L. "Paschal Mystery." In *The New Dictionary of Theology*, edited by Joseph A. Komonchak, Mary Collins, and Dermot A. Lane, 744–47. Collegeville, MN: Liturgical Press, 1987.

Francis, Mark R. "Remembrance." In *The Collegeville Pastoral Dictionary of Biblical Theology*, edited by Carroll Stuhlmueller and Dianne Bergant, 825. Collegeville, MN: Liturgical Press, 1996.

Francis, Pope. Address to Participants in the Plenary of the Pontifical Council for Promoting New Evangelization. October 14, 2013. https://w2.vatican.va/content/francesco/en/speeches/2013/october/documents/papa-francesco_20131014_plenaria-consiglio-nuova-evangelizzazione.html.

———. General Audience. May 11, 2016. https://w2.vatican.va/content/francesco/en/audiences/2016/documents/papa-francesco_20160511_udienza-generale.html.

———. Holy Mass and Canonization of Blessed Fr. Junípero Serra. September 23, 2015. https://w2.vatican.va/content/francesco/en/homilies/2015/documents/papa-francesco_20150923_usa-omelia-washington-dc.html.

———. Holy Mass for the 28th World Youth Day (Rio de Janeiro). July 28, 2013. http://w2.vatican.va/content/francesco/en/homilies/2013/documents/papa-francesco_20130728_celebrazione-xxviii-gmg.html.

———. The Face of Mercy (*Misericordiae Vultus*). Bull of Indiction of the Extraordinary Jubilee of Mercy. April 11, 2015. https://w2.vatican.va /content/francesco/en/apost_letters/documents/papa-francesco _bolla_20150411_misericordiae-vultus.html.

———. The Joy of the Gospel (*Evangelii Gaudium*). Apostolic Exhortation on the Proclamation of the Gospel in Today's World. November 24, 2013. http://w2.vatican.va/content/francesco/en/apost_exhortations /documents/papa-francesco_esortazione-ap_20131124_evangelii -gaudium.html.

———. Mass for the Possession of the Chair of the Bishop of Rome. April 7, 2013. https://w2.vatican.va/content/francesco/en/homilies/2013 /documents/papa-francesco_20130407_omelia-possesso-cattedra -laterano.html.

———. *The Name of God Is Mercy: A Conversation with Andrea Tornielli*. Translated by Oonagh Stransky. New York: Random House, 2016.

Hayes, Zachary. "Resurrection: Pastoral-Liturgical Tradition." In *The Collegeville Pastoral Dictionary of Biblical Theology*, edited by Carroll Stuhlmueller and Dianne Bergant, 839–41. Collegeville, MN: Liturgical Press, 1996.

Huebsch, Bill. "Parish Pastoral Planning Guide to Prepare for the Jubilee Year of Mercy." http://www.pastoralplanning.com/Jubilee/The _Medicine_of_Mercy_5_Meetings-sample.pdf.

John Paul II, Pope. Address to the United Nations. October 5, 1995. https:// w2.vatican.va/content/john-paul-ii/en/speeches/1995/october /documents/hf_jp-ii_spe_05101995_address-to-uno.html.

———. On Catechesis in Our Time (*Catechesi Tradendae*). Apostolic Exhortation. October 16, 1979.

Love, Larry. "A Reminder to Remember." Daily Democrat. July 7, 2012. https://www.dailydemocrat.com/social-affairs/20120707/a-reminder -to-remember.

MacFarquhar, Larissa. "When Giants Fail." *The New Yorker*. May 14, 2012. https://www.newyorker.com/magazine/2012/05/14/when-giants-fail.

Marthaler, Berard L. *The Creed: The Apostolic Faith in Contemporary Theology*. New London, CT: Twenty-Third Publications, 2007.

O'Collins, Gerald. "The Resurrection of Christ." In *The New Dictionary of Theology*, edited by Joseph A. Komonchak, Mary Collins, and Dermot A. Lane, 883. Collegeville, MN: Liturgical Press, 1987.

Paprocki, Joe. *Under the Influence of Jesus: The Transforming Experience of Encountering Christ*. Chicago: Loyola Press, 2014.

"Pope at Mass: Culture of Encounter Is the Foundation of Peace." *Vatican Radio*. May 22, 2013. http://en.radiovaticana.va/storico/2013/05/22 /pope_at_mass_culture_of_encounter_is_the_foundation_of_peace /en1-694445.

Rite of Christian Initiation of Adults. Study ed. Collegeville, MN: Liturgical Press, 1988.

Rome Reports. "Pope Says Phrase 'It's Always Done That Way' Damages the Church." *Romereports.com*. April 27, 2017. http://www.romereports .com/2017/04/27/pope-says-phrase-it-s-always-done-that-way -damages-the-church.

Scanlon, Michael J. "Revelation." In *The Modern Catholic Encyclopedia*, edited by Michael Glazier and Monika K. Hellwig, 748. Collegeville, MN: Liturgical Press, 2004.

Schreiter, Robert J. "Jesus Christ—Pastoral-Liturgical Tradition." In *The Collegeville Pastoral Dictionary of Biblical Theology*, edited by Carroll Stuhlmueller and Dianne Bergant, 488. Collegeville, MN: Liturgical Press, 1996.

Sinek, Simon. *Start with Why: How Great Leaders Inspire Everyone to Take Action*. London: Portfolio/Penguin, 2013.

Spadaro, Antonio. "A Big Heart Open to God: An Interview with Pope Francis." *America*. September 30, 2013. https://www.americamagazine .org/faith/2013/09/30/big-heart-open-god-interview-pope-francis.

United States Conference of Catholic Bishops. *United States Catholic Catechism for Adults*. Washington, DC: USCCB, 2006.

Vatican II Council. Decree on the Church's Missionary Activity (*Ad Gentes Divinitus*). December 7, 1965. In Austin Flannery, ed., *Vatican Council II: The Conciliar and Postconciliar Documents*. Collegeville, MN: Liturgical Press, 2014.

———. Dogmatic Constitution on Divine Revelation (*Dei Verbum*). November 18, 1965. In Austin Flannery, ed., *Vatican Council II: The Conciliar and Postconciliar Documents*. Collegeville, MN: Liturgical Press, 2014.

Wooden, Cindy. "Pope Francis' Constant Refrain: 'Go Forth,' Evangelize, Help the Poor." *Catholic News Service*. February 27, 2014. http://www

.catholicnews.com/services/englishnews/2014/pope-francis-constant
-refrain-go-forth-evangelize-help-the-poor.cfm.

Wormald, Benjamin. *U.S. Religious Landscape Survey: Religious Beliefs and
Practices.* Pew Research Center's Religion & Public Life project. June 1,
2008. http://www.pewforum.org/2008/06/01/u-s-religious-landscape
-survey-religious-beliefs-and-practices/.

XIII Ordinary General Assembly of the Synod of Bishops. Synodus Episco-
porum Bulletin. October 7–28, 2012. http://www.vatican.va/news
_services/press/sinodo/documents/bollettino_25_xiii-ordinaria-2012
/02_inglese/b33_02.html.

Yamane, David. *Becoming Catholic: Finding Rome in the American Religious
Landscape.* New York: Oxford University Press, 2014.